Let the Scriptures Speak

Let the Scriptures Speak

Reflections on the Sunday Readings, Year A

Dennis Hamm, S.J.

THE LITURGICAL PRESS
Collegeville, Minnesota

www.litpress.org

Cover design by Greg Becker.

Year A: ISBN 0-8146-2555-X
Year B: ISBN 0-8146-2556-8
Year C: ISBN 0-8146-2557-6

1   2   3   4   5   6   7   8

Library of Congress Cataloging-in-Publication Data

Hamm, M. Dennis.
    Let the scriptures speak : reflections on the Sunday readings,
  year B / Dennis Hamm.
        p.   cm.
    Includes bibliographical references.
    ISBN 0-8146-2556-8 (alk. paper)
    1. Church year meditations.   2. Common lectionary—Meditations.
  3. Bible—Liturgical lessons, English—Meditations.   4. Catholic
  Church—Prayer-books and devotions—English.   I. Title.
  BX2170.C55H35   1999
  242'.3—dc21   99-19050
                                                                      CIP

Contents

Introduction

For more than thirty years now, Catholics, as worshipers and preachers, have been stimulated and challenged in two ways by the renewal
of the Service of the Word in our Eucharistic Liturgy. First, Vatican II
mandated that the Lectionary should be revised so as to include a
richer variety of biblical readings. Second, the council mandated that
the sermon at Mass should be a biblical homily—an unfolding of Scripture, not simply a systematic exposition of doctrine or moral exhortation.

This enrichment of the liturgical readings and the mandate to preach
more biblically has challenged us all. For preachers, it has meant a
deeper and more constant study of Scripture. For all worshipers, as we
were exposed to the greater variety of readings during the Service of
the Word, it has called for greater attentiveness. And when preachers
have mounted the podium without first immersing themselves in
study of the biblical texts of the day, it has required tolerance and pa-
tience.

This situation has prompted the creation of many commentaries on
the three cycles of Sunday readings. Some of these commentaries come
in the form of homily helps, crib sheets for the harried pastor. Some of
these help expose each of the readings in an even-handed way, leaving
the application to the preacher. Others provide a little background on
the readings and then leap quickly to application. Some almost bypass
commentary on the texts, move quickly to a vivid anecdote, and rush
on to the application.

The reflections in this book take a different approach.

Realizing that the toughest challenge facing most of us, both as
preachers and worshipers, is to hear the readings afresh and with
understanding, my intent has been mainly to explain the readings. And
since the three Sunday readings and their accompanying psalm offer
more than one can fully absorb in one sitting, I have usually chosen to
focus on one of the readings and then to refer to the others insofar as they
complement what has caught my attention in the focus text. My first in-
terest is in the meaning of the text in the context of the document, and

in its original social context. For example, in explaining a passage from the letter to the Romans, I want first to hear what Paul meant by saying such a thing to that particular group of Christians gathered in that city at that time. My own experience is that the more I try to get at the meaning of the original author, the easier it is to hear how those words can have meaning for us today.

When it comes to the readings from the Old Testament, I have tried to hear first the original meaning in the context of the Hebrew Scriptures and then to appreciate the Christian reinterpretation of the Jewish text. When it comes to contemporary application, I mainly hint and suggest, for two reasons: the limitations of space and the conviction that application is a very personal thing.

Knowing that one can no more write others' homilies than pray their prayers, I have been content to write explanations and reflections on the Sunday readings, in the hope that they will help others pray and preach.

Most of these reflections appeared first as the column called "The Word" occupying the final page of *America,* the U.S. Jesuit journal of opinion. They follow the readings of Year A of the Liturgical Year and appeared in the issues of *America* from November 21, 1998, through November 13, 1999. Quite naturally, they occasionally allude to current events during that period (like the approach of Y2K or the impeachment process regarding President Clinton). Rather than delete these allusions or supply updated examples, I have let such references stand; usually the memories are still fresh and they often serve as reminders of other, more recent, parallels.

When I wrote these reflections for Year A in 1998–99, the feast of All Saints supplanted the 31st Sunday of the year. So I have written a reflection for that Sunday, as well as one for the Nativity of John the Baptist (June 24th), which falls on a Sunday in 2001. As it happens, in 2002 the first four Sundays of Lent will supplant the same four Sundays of the year as they did in 1999, the 8th through the 11th. That will not always be the case; so I have written fresh reflections for the 8th, 9th, 10th, and 11th Sundays in order that this series will fit any future occurrence of Year A. I have also added fresh reflections for Mary the Mother of God, Easter Sunday, and the Twentieth Sunday of the Year. I have retained the reflections for the date-linked feast of the Nativity of John the Baptist (June 24) and for the Assumption for the Blessed Virgin Mary (August 15).

(Those seeking ideas for other date-linked solemnities will find them treated in other volumes in this series. Five of them—the Presentation of the Lord [Feb. 2], Saints Peter and Paul [June 29], the Transfiguration [Aug. 6], All Souls Day [Nov. 2], and the Dedication of the Lateran

Basilica in Rome [Nov. 9]—are treated in the Year B volume of this series. And the volume for Year C includes reflections for All Saints [Nov. 1] as well as additional reflections for Mary, the Mother of God [Jan. 1] and the Epiphany [Jan. 6].)

I owe special thanks to the editors of *America* for inviting me to write the reflections and to those readers whose positive feedback encouraged me to offer this material for publication as a collection. Thanks, too, to The Liturgical Press for electing to publish the columns as a set of three volumes, one for each cycle. I am especially grateful to Dr. Mary Kuhlman, whose alert eye and canny ear saved me countless times from infelicitous and obscure expression.

Dennis Hamm, s.j.
Creighton University

First Sunday of Advent

Readings: Isa 2:1-5; Rom 13:11-14b; Matt 24:37-44

"They shall beat their swords into plowshares and their spears into pruning hooks." (Isa 2:4)

SWORDS INTO PLOWSHARES

If we were still using the dating system made popular by Hippolytus of Rome, we would be writing the year 7498 A.M. *(Anno Mundi)* in the upper right-hand corner of our correspondence. As it happens, we use the system devised by the sixth-century monk Dionysius Exiguus ("Tiny Dennis"), who advised that it would be more apt for Christian Europe to place the incarnation at the center of history and to date events prior to Christ by counting backward, leaving the normal forward count for the events after that first Advent. It took the promotion of another monk, Venerable Bede, a century and a half later, to popularize that dating system. And we have been living with the B.C./A.D. (or, frequently today, B.C.E./C.E.) system ever since.

Accordingly, this first Sunday of Advent begins a Church Year that will usher us up to the edge of the beginning of the third millennium C.E. The Y2K computer bug and prophecies of doom notwithstanding, the approach of the third millennium should, in the eyes of faith, simply serve to remind us what the season of Advent has always been about. For the Church, the year 2000 will simply be a special jubilee year, doing what jubilee years have always done. The millennial turn will mark a special anniversary of the incarnation, celebrating the new beginning signaled by the First Advent of Christ, and occasioning repentance and renewed commitment to the good work that God has begun among us in Jesus.

Advent has always been a miniature of such anniversary jubilees. During this time, we focus our prayer and our liturgy on how we, and the rest of the world, continue to hunger for the dream that the incarnation,

1

two millennia ago, began to realize. The language for expressing the hope that the first Advent began to implement was supplied in great part by the authors of the scroll of Isaiah. This Sunday's first reading gives us one of the most powerful articulations of that hope.

If you visit the Old City of Jerusalem and stand on the Temple Mount and look around, the imagery of Isaiah 2 takes on the dramatic edge it was meant to have. You find yourself standing on the hill the Bible calls Zion. It is a conspicuous shoulder of earth, to be sure, but it is noticeably *lower* than the mountains and hills surrounding it. So when you read, "In the days to come, the mountain of the Lord's house shall be established as the highest mountain and raised above the hills," you know that you are reading an apocalyptic vision. That is, you are reading a description of an event that is not of human making. It is a work of "earth-shaking" proportions brought about by divine intervention. Further, this vision of the end-times pictures all nations acknowledging Yahweh as the one God and king of all. They are streaming to Zion to learn Torah as a means of living in international peace. People will be moved to turn instruments of war, like swords and spears, into implements of peace, like agricultural tools such as plowshares and pruning hooks. (It is poignant to read that vision just now, when rival political claimants to present-day Zion are still laboring to move beyond violence to make Jerusalem a place of *shalom*.)

That Jesus and the early Christians took this vision seriously is clear from the New Testament. Jesus called his followers "the light of the world." He compared them to a city on a hill, whose lights are visible for miles around. He blessed the makers of peace and challenged his disciples to find nonviolent ways of responding to violence. He even went so far as to advocate loving one's enemies and praying for one's persecutors. If this sounds like raising Zion above the surrounding landscape (moving mountains), that is as it should be. Such peacemaking is, finally, not something people do on their own. It is something that God does with and through them.

Advent comes to remind us that what the human heart most deeply desires, God began to fulfill in the first Advent—the life, death, and resurrection of Jesus of Nazareth. And what God has begun in Christ Jesus, God will complete—if those touched by this good news allow themselves to be used for such apocalyptic (read "humanly unrealistic but divinely possible") peacemaking.

Second Sunday of Advent

Readings: Isa 11:1-10; Rom 15:4-9; Matt 3:1-12

"In him shall all the tribes of the earth be blessed."
(Ps 72:17)

THE WINNOWER

John the baptizer confronted his peers like the prophets of old, with imagery drawn from the agricultural life around them—wind, fire, water, and the ax laid to the root. Nothing was more familiar than the sight of farmers winnowing their grain. First they would thresh the grain to break down the kernels into their components of wheat and chaff, which of course remained a mix in need of sorting. That step took place on a windy day, when they would heave forkfuls of grain into the air and the breeze would separate the good stuff from the useless. The lighter chaff would be blown off to the side, and the heavier wheat would drop back to the ground in a precious pile. Later, the chaff would be swept up and burned. Thus the grain harvest was a matter of gathering and sorting with the help of wind and fire. The fact that the same word, *ruach,* meant both wind and spirit made it easy to use that threshing and winnowing process as a powerful metaphor for the ultimate sorting of divine judgment.

The imagery becomes multilayered when John says of the one who is to come, "He will baptize you in the Holy Spirit and fire." On the one hand, the image alludes to the sorting process of threshing, evoking the decisiveness of divine judgment. On the other hand, the words recall the promise of end-time renewal, especially as expressed in the oracles of Ezekiel and Joel. Reference to immersion in the Spirit recalls Ezekiel's words: "I will sprinkle clean water upon you to cleanse you from all your impurities . . . I will put my spirit within you, and make you live by my statutes, be careful to observe my decrees. You shall live in the land I gave your fathers; you shall be my people, and I will be

3

your God" (36:25-28). Later, Joel spoke of God pouring out his spirit on all flesh—on sons and daughters, old and young, even on the male and female slaves (3:1-5).

It is possible that the historical John focused on the theme of judgment, whereas the post-Easter Church could highlight the pentecostal fulfillment of Spirit and fire. The coming of the kingdom of God entails both renewal and judgment as aspects of the one reality of God's special intervention in the Age to Come.

In the Baptist's view, what especially deserved divine judgment was complacency in privilege: "And do not presume to say to yourselves, 'We have Abraham as our father.' For I tell you, God can raise up children to Abraham from these stones." "Give some evidence that you mean to reform," he tells them. From the story of Abraham forward, the Hebrew Scriptures insist that Israel was chosen to benefit the nations. Privilege was meant for universal service. The People of God have a mission to be a light for the nations. Our Christian claim is that we take as our own that universal vocation of Israel.

Each of this Sunday's readings touches on that theme. Isaiah's vision of peace pictures the Davidic king set up as a signal for the nations which the Gentiles seek out. Psalm 72 applies the promise to Abraham to God's anointed one: "May the tribes of the earth give blessings with his name." And Paul, addressing the human division that most challenged the Christians of Rome, urged, "Welcome one another, then, as Christ welcomed you, for the glory of God. For, I say that Christ became a minister of the circumcized to show of God's truthfulness, to confirm the promises to the patriarchs, but so that the Gentiles might glorify God for his mercy."

A report I heard on the radio this morning spoke of a Harvard research project on race and hypertension. The data show that black people, as they age, suffer more from hypertension than whites. The hypothesis of the researchers is that, given the genetic diversity of African Americans, the likeliest common factor to account for this statistic is the stress that black people experience due to racism. Ironically, as biological science discovers the category of race to be increasingly meaningless, social science shows that the mental construction of race is very real indeed, especially in its negative expression as racism.

If we who claim the privilege of being the People of God, a signal to the nations, wonder how the Baptist's wake-up call might apply to us, we might ask whether we have fully addressed racism, even within the community of the Church. The God of all nations, the one whose spirit sorts the wheat from the chaff, is also the one who offers the spirit and fire of renewal.

Third Sunday of Advent

Readings: Isa 35:1-6a, 10; Jas 5:7-10; Matt 11:2-11

"Are you the one who is to come, or should we look for another?" (Matt 11:3)

A HEALING MESSIAH?

John the Baptizer, in prison because of his confrontation with Herod over the king's unlawful marriage, sends disciples to ask Jesus if he really is the one they have been expecting. That action triggers one of the most fascinating exchanges in the Gospels.

Matthew makes it clear that there is no question in his own mind as to the identity of Jesus. He writes: "When John heard in prison of *the works of the Messiah*, he sent his disciples to him . . ." (New American Bible, 1986). In other words, from his post-Easter perspective, Matthew has no trouble referring to Jesus as "the Christ." But the Baptist apparently had his doubts. Why? Among the varieties of Judaisms of the first century—among, for example, Pharisees, Sadducees, Essenes—there was a corresponding variety of images of the Messiah. Some expected the Anointed One to emerge from the priestly caste. Others looked for a prophet like Moses. Many expected a son of David cut from the same combative cloth, i.e., a warrior king who would defeat their enemies and establish political autonomy for the people of Judea. John had preached a coming Judgment Day, when the ax would be laid to the root.

Along comes Jesus, telling stories, eating with sinners, and healing. While is it possible that John knew perfectly well that Jesus was the Messiah, and, as a pedagogical ploy, was simply setting his disciples up to discover that for themselves, it is plausible that the question of Jesus' identity was very much his own.

As is typical of Jesus when confronted with a question, he prompts the questioners to discover the answer for themselves. Rather than giving a simple yes or no, Jesus instructs them to tell John what they see and hear. He proceeds to describe what they are seeing and hearing in words that echo Isaiah. The mention of blind people seeing, lame persons walking and deaf people hearing evokes the very passage used as our first reading this Sunday (Isa 35:1-6). And the reference to preaching Good News to the poor recalls Isaiah 61. As far as we know, no one in Judea at this time expected that the coming Anointed One would be a healer.

In effect, then, Jesus was telling John's disciples: "Look around and see what is happening. The healings that Isaiah links with the end-time restoration of Israel are happening. Just maybe, the 'One who is to come' at the end-time is here as well." In the next chapter Jesus makes it clear that his healings and his messianic mission are connected: "If it is by the Spirit of God that I drive out demons, then the kingdom of God has come upon you" (12:28).

These healings of the blind, deaf, and lame that made up so much of the ministries of Jesus and the early Church—were they simply signs to prove the divinity of Jesus and special helps for the infant Christian communities? Some authors have thought so. But there is also a long tradition of interpretation, including many patristic writers, who understand the healing portrayed in the New Testament as a normal component of Church life. The Church's requirement of documented healing miracles in the canonization process is an indication that healing beyond medical explanation is a continued expectation in the Church. The ongoing documentation of extraordinary physical healings at Lourdes is another reminder.

Yet these extraordinary experiences can distract us from the reality that healing, mental and physical, has always been a side effect of the life of faith lived fully. The patristic writings refer to healing in response to prayer as a fact of Church life. Testimonies regarding physical and mental healings in the context of contemporary prayer groups abound. My own suspicion is that most common (undocumented) healing occurs when a mother prays for an ailing child. And isn't it true that all of our daily personal encounters are either a little bit healing or a little bit toxic? It is good to remember that the risen Lord we approach and mediate in the sacraments is a healing Messiah. Openness to that reality can be a source of wholeness in our personal and collective lives.

Fourth Sunday of Advent

Readings: Isa 7:10-14; Rom 1:1-7; Matt 1:18-24

**"She will bear a son and you are to name him Jesus,
because he will save his people from their sins."
(Matt 1:21)**

JOSEPH'S DREAM

The message of Christmas is so simple and powerful—the eternal Word of God becomes our kind of flesh—that we can easily slide unthinkingly over some of the surprising preliminaries. An example is Joseph's dilemma and its resolution by a dream. Here is a good Jewish man engaged to be married, and he learns that his bride has become pregnant before they have come together. The Law, specifically Deuteronomy 22:23-27, treats such a fact as adultery and calls for the stoning to death of the engaged woman and the guilty male. As a keeper of the Law, Joseph realizes that, given the apparent facts, he must divorce Mary (though death by stoning does not seem a likely outcome at this time). But rather than expose her to the shame of public trial, he decides to divorce her privately. Before he gets a chance to do this, however, he has a dream in which the angel of the Lord tells him that the conception is by the Holy Spirit. Further, he is told to name the child *Jesus* "because he will save his people from their sins."

That choice of name is no casual thing. It is both more fitting and more surprising than we might think. *Jesus* is the Greek form of a Hebrew name, *Jeshua* or *Jehoshua* (Joshua in English), commonly interpreted "Yahweh saves." Ordinarily, if parents gave it a second thought, calling their baby Joshua meant that they were naming the child after the great Israelite leader of the conquest of Canaan. In addition, the name celebrated the real agent of the Exodus/Conquest, or any other salvation event—God. Now comes the surprising part. The message to Joseph explains the name by saying that *he*, Jesus himself, will save his

7

people. Moreover, the kind of saving involved in this case is not the usual military kind of saving, i.e., from *enemies*, like the Egyptians of old or the Romans in their own day. No, it is far more radical than that; he will save his people *from their sins.*

We are so accustomed to that message to Joseph that we miss the astounding claim that this child will perform a divine act of saving and that the saving will be from nothing less than sin itself. That should stop us in our Advent tracks. Nothing like that was ever said of any Old Testament hero. This is a claim of divine presence as bold as the prologue of the Fourth Gospel. If we are in any doubt that Matthew means us to hear it that way, his own comment in the next verse confirms it.

Matthew finds in Isaiah 7 words that, applied to Jesus, leap beyond their original context. Isaiah, in his day, was speaking of a young woman giving birth and naming her child Immanuel. Matthew delights in the fact that the Greek Bible translates *almah* ("young woman") with *parthenos* ("virgin"), thereby making the words an especially apt description of Jesus' origin. What is more, the name given to the child in Isaiah 7, Immanuel ("With-us-God"), applies to Jesus in a way neither Isaiah nor Ahaz, his interlocutor, could have guessed. Let's linger with the wonder of the message to Joseph as we move toward the celebration of God come to save us from our sins in the flesh of Jesus.

Christmas Day

Readings: Isa 52:7-10; Heb 1:1-6; John 1:1-18

> **"How beautiful upon the mountains**
> **are the feet of him who brings glad tidings,**
> **announcing peace, bearing good news,**
> **announcing salvation, and saying to Zion,**
> **'Your God is King!'" (Isa 52:7)**

EXILE'S END

If Matthew makes bold to claim up front that the birth of the child Jesus is the presence of God come to save us, the readings for Christmas Day, from the letter to the Hebrews and the Gospel of John, proclaim the same thing in even broader strokes.

Hebrews shout that Jesus of Nazareth is the climax of the Creator's communication to his people: "In times past, God spoke in partial and various ways to our ancestors through the prophets; in these last days, he has spoken to us through a Son, whom he made heir of all things and through whom he created the universe." The remainder of that magnificent introduction goes on to say that the fullness of that communication through the eternal Son came to expression in his death and exaltation.

The prologue of John says the same thing more fully by calling Jesus the fullness of life, light for the darkness, eternal Word enfleshed, the very tenting of God in our midst.

We read Isaiah 52 today because we know that the end to exile which that prophet called good news has occurred supremely in the coming of Christ Jesus.

The Holy Family of Jesus, Mary, and Joseph

Readings: Sir 3:2-6, 2-14; Col 3:12-21; Matt 2:13-15, 19-23

> **"He who reveres his father will live a long life;**
> **he obeys the LORD who brings comfort to his mother."**
> **(Sir 3:6)**

IT TAKES A COVENANT TO RAISE A FAMILY

The Holy Family—so easy to marvel at and honor, so difficult to think of imitating. On the face of it, the family life of Jesus, Mary, and Joseph seems too utterly unique to take as a model for our flawed efforts at being parents and children. The virginal conception and divinity of the Child are enough to render the holy family apparently inimitable. And who among us can hope for guidance in major decisions by way of angelic messages in dreams? And yet, I submit, this Sunday's Scriptures do offer ways for us to relate the life of Jesus, Mary, and Joseph to our own.

When we think of Mary, Joseph, and the child Jesus in splendid, nuclear isolation, we forget two things. First, no family in first-century Palestine lived disconnected from their network of relatives. Second, and more important, their family life was lived as part of the larger family life of Israel's covenant life with God.

The passage from Sirach demonstrates the way Israelite family life was considered an expression of covenant life. Each statement Sirach makes about living the parent-child relationships refers to what those relationships mean about one's relationship with God. Indeed, those relationships are described in liturgical terms. For example, "He who honors his father is gladdened by children, and when he prays he is heard." Or again, "He obeys the LORD who brings comfort to his mother."

However divine conception and direction by dreams highlights their uniqueness, Jesus, Mary and Joseph had in common with all the families in the land of Israel this sense that their relationships with one another were expressions of their relationship with Yahweh as creator and redeemer. With all of their neighbors, they knew that it takes a covenant community to be a family, and that their lives were the gift of God to be lived out in service of that God. Matthew can quote Hosea 11:1, "Out of Egypt I called my son," not only because the words take on powerful new meaning when applied to Jesus. Another powerful aspect of that quotation is what it carries forward from its original context in Hosea. The prophet is speaking of the Exodus redemption from bondage in Egypt and is calling the entire people of Israel (men and women both, of course) *child and son of God*. When these words are applied to Jesus, they refer not only to his unique sonship but also to the fact that he embodies the renewal of the whole people's covenant "sonship" with God. As Jesus renews that covenant, he renews the family life that is part of that covenant.

When Paul speaks of right relationships in Christian community and family life, he draws upon that same sense that these human relationships derive from that larger covenant relationship. "As the Lord has forgiven you, so must you also do." "And let the peace of Christ control your hearts, the peace into which you were also called in our body." That peace is the *shalom* of the covenant life lived faithfully and fully. It takes the whole covenant community to be a family. As we honor the Holy Family today, we can take their unique experience as a reminder of the covenant life with God in which all of our families can find encouragement. Just as Mary, Joseph, and Jesus were not a family on their own, neither are we.

Mary, the Mother of God
(January 1)

Readings: Num 6:22-27; Gal 4:4-7; Luke 2:16-21

> **"As proof that you are children, God sent the spirit of
> his Son into our hearts, crying out, 'Abba, Father!'
> So you are no longer a slave but a child, and if a child
> then also an heir, through God." (Gal 4:6-7)**

If we take seriously the incarnation, along with the full divine "emptying out" it entails (Phil 2:7), we can wonder at how the child Jesus was nurtured in his Jewish faith. Given the culture of that time and place, where the child was first nurtured in the mother's world and then initiated by the father into the world of men, Jesus most likely learned to pray in Mary's lap. It is not too great a speculative leap to conjecture that Jesus' striking way of addressing the Creator with the intimate term Abba was also something he learned from his mother. What a powerful testimony to the power of a mother's intimate moments with her child that Paul, decades later, could refer to that Abba-prayer as something the Gentile Christians of Galatia would recognize as their usual way of praying. Thinking of this may enrich our own recitation of the Lord's Prayer.

Epiphany of the Lord (January 6)

Readings: Isa 60:1-6; Eph 3:2-3a, 5-6; Matt 2:1-12

> ". . . I suppose, you have heard of the stewardship of
> God's grace that was given to me for your benefit,
> [namely, that] the mystery was made known to me by
> revelation, . . . that the Gentiles are coheirs, members
> of the same body, and copartners in the promise in
> Christ Jesus through the gospel." (Eph 3:2, 6)

WE GENTILES

It is safe to say that any group of U.S. Catholics gathered to worship on this feast is a congregation of Gentiles expressing the faith that Jesus of Nazareth is the Messiah of Israel and our own Lord and savior. If there is ever a time in the Liturgical Year when we should acknowledge our connection with the people of historic Israel and our participation in their faith in a creating and redeeming God, it is on the feast of the Epiphany.

For centuries, we Gentile messianists managed to live comfortably with imagery that pictured the Israelite tradition to be the discarded husk of Christianity, something that could be symbolized in Renaissance paintings as ancient architectural ruins comprising the grey background of the Christian foreground. Fortunately, we now live in a moment of Church history enlightened by the teaching of Vatican II on the matter of our relationship with Judaism. In *Nostra aetate* (The Declaration of the Relationship of the Church to Non-Christian Religions, 1965), the teaching Church, drawing on the wisdom of the New Testament, spoke fresh words to our contemporary context of religious pluralism. It is an appropriate moment to reflect on some of its words.

Consider, for example, this, from section four, on Judaism: "The church cannot forget that it received the revelation of the Old Testament by way of that people with whom God in his inexpressible mercy

13

established the ancient covenant. Nor can it forget that it draws nourishment from the good olive tree onto which the wild olive branches of the Gentiles have been grafted (see Rom 11:17-24)." Epiphany is a good time to remember our roots and the covenant never revoked, for as Paul said regarding his fellow Jews, "The gifts and the call of God are irrevocable" (Rom 11:29).

Baptism of the Lord

Readings: Isa 42:1-4, 6-7; Acts 10:34-38; Matt 3:13-17

"He shall bring forth justice to the nations." (Isa 42:1)

A PEACE CHURCH?

"Are they trying to make the Catholic Church a peace church?" This sentiment was among the reactions to the pastoral letter that our U.S. bishops issued fifteen years ago called *The Challenge of Peace* (1983). I recall finding that response provocative and illuminating. I knew what the speaker meant: there are Christian denominations such as the Quakers and Mennonites that have made peacemaking and even pacifism a dominant theme in their devotion and action; and no historian has ever grouped Roman Catholics in that category. But as soon as I recognized that fact, I had to ask, "Why not?" Is not peacemaking central to the teaching of Jesus? There was no doubt of that in our bishops' minds when they wrote their peace pastoral. And they were echoing powerful statements from recent popes. ("If you want peace, work for justice," said Pope Paul VI.) Each of this Sunday's readings invites us to ponder the centrality of peace and justice in the mission of Jesus and in the mission of any of us who claim to be his disciples.

The selection from Isaiah contains the famous figure of the Servant of Yahweh. Commentators have debated long and hard whether this servant stands for Israel as a whole or for an individual within Israel. The consensus now is that, in the full context of Isaiah 40–55, the servant stands for both; that is, the figure of the servant represents Israel in her mission to be a light to the nations, and at the same time the language points to the role of a person within Israel who enables her to fulfill that mission. The poem is written as a divine oracle, and the words promise a special endowment of the spirit of God, thus marking the mission as prophetic. It is also in the language of kingship ("establishing justice on the earth"), with the startling difference that this reign

15

will come about not through military conquest but through conspicuously nonviolent means ("a bruised reed he shall not break, / and a smoldering wick he shall not quench").

The Gospel account of the baptism of the Lord alludes to this passage from Isaiah by combining the descent of the spirit of God with the divine voice's reference to the Son "with whom I am well pleased" (Matt 3:17; Isa 42:1). Against this background, the exchange between John the Baptist and Jesus, unique to Matthew's account, makes profound sense. Attempting to prevent Jesus from joining the conversion ritual, John says, "I need to be baptized by you, and yet you are coming to me?" To which Jesus replies, "Allow it now, for thus it is fitting for us to fulfill all righteousness." Does this exchange recall otherwise neglected sayings of John? More likely, it is an expansion by Matthew, answering a doubt some may have had about the propriety of the Baptist seeming to have a superior role here. The clarification is profound: the question of superiority is secondary to the fact that each is "fulfilling all righteousness"—a word special to Matthew's Jewish vocabulary meaning to do the will of God. Here righteousness means especially to carry out the peace and justice mission articulated in the Servant passage echoed by the heavenly voice. It is the righteousness spelled out concretely in the Sermon on the Mount (see Matt 5:6, 10, 20; 6:33), where Jesus clearly calls his followers to nonviolence and love of enemies.

When Luke summarizes the meaning of the baptism of the Lord in the speech of Peter to Cornelius's household in Acts, he draws on this same portrait of the Servant in Isaiah. "You know the word [that God] sent to the Israelites as he proclaimed peace through Jesus Christ, who is Lord of all, what has happened all over Judea, beginning in Galilee after the baptism that John preached, how God anointed Jesus of Nazareth with the holy Spirit and power" (Acts 10:36-38).

The thrust of this biblical teaching suggests that any community calling itself Christian is necessarily called to be, in a profound sense, a peace church. Our Pope and bishops have been trying to call our attention to this for some time now.

Second Sunday of the Year

Readings: Isa 49:3, 5-6; 1 Cor 1:1-3; John 1:29-34

**"I will make you a light to the nations,
that my salvation may reach to the ends of the earth."
(Isa 49:6)**

THIS LITTLE LIGHT OF MINE

Some years ago, I was attending a farewell party for a rabbinic scholar about to take a professorship at a state university. At one point he said, "Yes, I am going to be *or le goyim*." Even those of us whose Hebrew was rusty knew exactly what he meant. *Or le goyim* is a phrase from Isaiah meaning "a light to the Gentiles (or nations)." Appearing in this Sunday's reading from Isaiah (Isa 49:6), as well as last Sunday's (Isa 42:6), it refers to the divinely mandated mission of Servant Israel. The phrase is a consecrated one, not only within the Jewish tradition but also in the Christian, for early on we claimed its fulfillment in Jesus and the Church (see Luke 2:32 and Acts 13:47; 26:23).

"Light to the nations" highlights another theme sounded by our Church as we approach the millennial jubilee—evangelization. It may not be obvious at first glance, but all of this Sunday's readings point in that direction.

When John the Baptizer heralds Jesus as the one who baptizes "with the Holy Spirit," he is referring to the fact that Jesus is the agent fulfilling Israel's hope for renewal through a divine outpouring of the Holy Spirit, as expressed especially in Ezekiel 36:24-27 and Joel 3:1-5. How this entails mission becomes evident later in John's Gospel when the risen Lord appears to the disciples and says, "As the Father has sent me, so I send you," and then breathes on them, saying, "Receive the holy Spirit." Being born again in water and the Holy Spirit entails furthering Jesus' mission of being the "light of the world" (in the language of John 9:5 regarding Jesus himself, or of Matthew 5:14 regarding followers of Jesus) and a "light to the nations" (in the language we have been reviewing in Isaiah and Luke).

When Paul, in this Sunday's second reading, addresses the Christians of Corinth as "called to be holy," he is alluding to their status as heirs of the vocation of Israel. And when he refers to them as those "who call upon the name of our Lord," he is applying to them a phrase from that Spirit passage of Joel 3. As people baptized in the Spirit and sharing the vocation of Israel, they are of course meant to be a "light to the nations." We read these ancient passages in our worshiping communities because we claim that vocation for ourselves.

Third Sunday of the Year

Readings: Isa 8:23–9:3; 1 Cor 1:10-13, 17; Matt 4:12-23

**"He said to them, 'Come after me, and
I will make you fishers of men.'" (Matt 4:19)**

GOOD WILL FISHING

For many years, "fishing for people" seemed to me an odd and dangerous way to describe the apostolic mission. First, fishing is a predator-prey activity, perfectly legitimate in the larger scheme of things in which humans use fish to feed their need for protein, but clearly bad news for the fish. And then there are those phrases in our language that link fishing imagery with devious human activity. We speak disapprovingly, for example, of someone "fishing" for a compliment. Or we refer to the sinister work of drug pushers as getting people "hooked." The work of another kind of hooker is sometimes described as "luring." How does an image that has such negative connotations fit the ministry to which Jesus calls his followers?

For starters, the connotations that fishing imagery has in current English are not necessarily the associations people would have made in first-century Palestine. While archaeologists have indeed found what appear to be ancient fishhooks around the Sea of Galilee, the Gospel references to fishing envision the net technique, as with the nets used by Peter and Andrew and the brothers Zebedee in today's Gospel. Already we have moved from hooking to gathering. Further, some have found in the ancient world a use of the fishing image to refer to bringing people to a new level of consciousness, analogous to moving from underwater existence to open-air existence (fatal to gill-breathers, of course, but a positive move for humans).

More pertinent perhaps, because more biblical, is the possible background of Jeremiah 16:16—"I will send many fishermen, says the LORD, to catch them." How is this to be taken? If the statement goes with what follows that verse, hunting out evildoers, the fishing is a kind of "search-and-destroy" action. If, however, the verse goes with what precedes it ("I will bring them back to their own land that I gave to their ancestors"), then the fishing image refers to the ingathering of restoration after exile. If that is the meaning of "fishers of men" in Jesus' saying, the phrase integrates powerfully with his preaching about the coming kingdom of God. For the coming of the reign of God means the end of the spiritual exile that the people of Israel felt they had been experiencing for centuries. Understood this way, the call to fish for people was an invitation to join Jesus in his preaching and enactment of the coming reign of God (or "kingdom of heaven," in Matthew's preferred phrase).

If we wonder how this mission applies to Church life today, our first thoughts might very rightly run to our ongoing mission of evangelization. But the second reading, from Paul to the Corinthians, suggests another kind of unfinished apostolic business—healing divisions within the Church. The Corinthians are indulging in rivalries that threaten the unity of the body of Christ. Having been unified by baptism and faith, they are now allowing factions to pull them apart. The gathered people are allowing themselves to be scattered. Paul answers by reminding them that this motley crowd were first gathered into unity by their discovery of the power and wisdom of God in Christ crucified and in the life of mutual service to which that discovery drew them.

We need not look far to find analogies to Paul's Corinthian community in our Church today. Our Church knows increasing polarization that can be described in a multitude of ways: e.g., between those who are attracted by the late Cardinal Bernardin's call for Catholics to recover our "common ground," and those who find such talk a threat to orthodoxy; between those who like their Gospel served on The Eternal Word Network and those who do not; between those who find the word of God in revelations at Medjugorje and those who are content with the mainstream tradition and magisterium; between those who find a kinship with the "Christian right" and those who find in that alignment a serious neglect of the common good.

Each of us could compose our own list, finding our emotional heat rising with each entry. The Church has always carried, and probably always will carry, creative and painful tension in its body. But as Paul and Matthew remind us, what we have in common is that, like the Corinthians, we have found Jesus to be light in darkness; we have dropped the nets of the world's business-as-usual. We who have been summoned to gather others into new life are called to work out our own differences in ways that serve the body of the Church and enable that body to serve the world.

Fourth Sunday of the Year

Readings: Zeph 2:3; 3:12-13; 1 Cor 1:26-31; Matt 5:1-12a

> **"Blessed are the poor in spirit,**
> **for theirs is the kingdom of heaven." (Matt 5:3)**

POOR IN SPIRIT

Who are the poor in spirit? Several common misunderstandings can block our comprehension of the first Beatitude. For example, some people hear the phrase "poor in spirit" as analogous with language like "the soil is poor in nitrogen"—as if the condition of being relatively spirit-less were being praised. This misunderstanding springs from an unfortunate accident of language. Then there is the reading that takes the first Beatitude as a consolation of the destitute, as if Jesus were saying to the economically deprived, "Don't worry: you are suffering now in your poverty, but your present suffering will be amply recompensed in the next life, after you die." But "kingdom of heaven" is simply Matthew's Jewish way of referring to what is elsewhere in the Gospels called "the kingdom of God," or God's reign, already inaugurated in the life of Jesus and accessible even before death.

Another source of confusion, common even in commentaries, is the claim that Luke's version, "Blessed are (you) poor," congratulates the economically destitute, whereas Matthew's version somehow takes the bite out of the Beatitude by "spiritualizing" it with the phrase "in spirit."

The case can be made that *both* Luke and Matthew are faithful to the teaching of Jesus, which draws its meaning of "the poor" from Isaiah. In a number of places, Isaiah describes Israel in exile as poor, hungry, mourning as they await God's response to their need for rescue from exile. In this context, to be poor is to know your need for God.

Once we are in touch with the biblical home base of "the poor," we can see why Matthew introduced the phrase "in spirit," for knowing one's need for God is a disposition of the heart, not an economic state.

At the same time, however, those who know the pinch of actual poverty have the edge in knowing their need for God. In this respect, the economically secure can more easily succumb to the delusion that they are self-sufficient.

How, then, do those of us who are relatively secure economically qualify for the blessing of the "poor in spirit"? Some have found that poverty of spirit by discovering their helplessness in the experience of addiction or in the loss of a loved one. Others have learned to recover their need for God by standing in solidarity with the economically deprived and seeing the world anew through their eyes.

Fifth Sunday of the Year

Readings: Isa 58:7-10; 1 Cor 2:1-5; Matt 5:13-16

"You are the light of the world." (Matt 5:14)

BEING LIGHT, UNIMPEACHABLY

When Jesus calls his followers "the light of the world," he speaks out of a powerful prophetic tradition. The Hebrew prophet of the Babylonian Exile whom we call Second Isaiah articulated that image of Israel's vocation memorably when he called Servant/Israel "a light for the nations" (Isa 42:6; 49:6). Later, in the reading we hear today, a later, post-exilic prophet we call Third Isaiah gave a new precision to that image. This prophet draws a precise connection between meeting human needs and both *finding* light and *becoming* light. The words are worth quoting in full:

> *Thus says the LORD:*
> *[Share] your bread with the hungry,*
> * [shelter] the oppressed and the homeless;*
> *[Clothe] the naked when you see them,*
> * and [do not turn] your back on your own.*
> *Then your light shall break forth like the dawn,*
> * and your wound shall quickly be healed . . .*

Further, to make sure we do not miss his meaning, just a few verses later Isaiah writes:

> *If you remove from your midst oppression,*
> * false accusation and malicious speech;*
> *If you bestow your bread on the hungry*
> * and satisfy the afflicted;*
> *Then light shall rise for you in the darkness,*
> * and the gloom shall become for you like midday.*

As I write this column, we are impeaching our president. Some see this as the magisterial working out of our constitutional process. Others see it as an irresponsible and vindictive abuse of legislative, executive, and judicial time, talent, and treasure. Meanwhile, the bombing of Iraq is treated as a mere sidebar (euphemistically described as "degrading Saddam's program"), while the loss of civilian life is dismissed as "collateral damage."

However one interprets these actions, issues crying out for action on the level of public policy go unaddressed. For example, it has been observed that even as our economy, judged by some indexes, appears to be flourishing, the gap between rich and poor continues to grow.

Someone has described our situation in the following terms. Imagine our nation as a group of five families and our collective earnings as a hundred dollars. The wealthiest of the five takes home $47 and the poorest of the five is left with $3.60 (down from $4.60 a decade ago). Meanwhile, as family no. 1 grows richer and family no. 5 poorer, what the middle family takes home, around $17, has scarcely changed in a quarter century. Is this not a matter deserving of legislative, executive, and judicial attention? One suspects that Isaiah and Jesus would say so. Our Pope and bishops have tried to alert us to this injustice.

If we seek healing and release from malicious speech, and if we hope to find light and even become a light to others, the mandate of Isaiah to attend to human needs still rings loud and clear.

Sixth Sunday of the Year

Readings: Sir 15:15-20; 1 Cor 2:6-10; Matt 5:17-37

> **"I tell you, unless your righteousness surpasses that of the scribes and Pharisees, you will not enter into the kingdom of heaven." (Matt 5:20)**

With this Sunday's Gospel reading, we move into the part of the Sermon on the Mount that scholars call the six antitheses. The label intends to highlight the fact that here, six times in a row, the words of Jesus follow a pattern that goes, "You have heard that it was said. . . . But I say to you . . ." Here we meet Jesus asserting an authority even greater than Moses. In our awe, we can miss the bite and challenge of Jesus' words.

As an ear-opening exercise, let's listen carefully to what Jesus says in the antithesis about murder. He begins by citing the commandment and its consequence: *whoever kills will be liable to judgment.* "Judgment" here is not punishment after death but a reference to the juridical process of a trial. The law says, "Kill and you shall be tried for it." Jesus then asserts, *But I say to you, whoever is angry with his brother will be liable to judgment.*

At this point the rational listener is supposed to say, "Wait a minute! You can't litigate about anger. There's no deed, no action to take to court." Jesus' implied answer is, "Right. Don't think you are obeying the Torah on murder just because you haven't killed. I am calling you to something that the law can't reach, the disposition of your heart. If you want to forestall violence, deal with the anger in your heart." If we catch the point of this first example, the meaning of the rest of the verse falls into place. *And whoever says to his brother, 'Raqa,' will be answerable to the Sanhedrin, and whoever says, 'You fool,' will be liable to fiery Gehenna.* "Raqa" is an insult term like our "airhead," and already we are standing before the Jerusalem Supreme Court! "You fool" is still in the realm of trash talk, not violent action, and now the consequence has escalated to damnation. This is parody. Jesus is imitating the language of legalistic calibration matching punishment to crime, all to the same point: "I am challenging you to a purity of heart that the calculus of the law cannot reach. So don't be complacent that you haven't killed yet."

In short, Jesus does not make new laws; for living the law, he brings a new vision and a new help—a refreshed covenant relationship with God.

Ash Wednesday

Readings: Joel 2:12-18; 2 Cor 5:20–6:2; Matt 6:1-6, 16-18

> **"So we are ambassadors for Christ, as if God were appealing through us. We implore you on behalf of Christ, be reconciled to God." (2 Cor 5:20)**

This year, the Ash Wednesday readings, coming on the heels of the Cycle-A readings of the Fifth Sunday of the Year, ring with a new urgency. How are we to act responsibly in a world grown increasingly violent, unjust, partisan, and mean-spirited? Not, surely, by securing our own little corner. Not by making preemptive strikes against a likely enemy, for then we turn likely enemies into actual and active ones. Not by concentrating on protecting "our own," for our own remain vulnerable in a world unreconciled. Joel, Jesus, and Paul call us to attend to our relationship with the Creator of us all. Echoing Joel, Paul commands his distracted Corinthians, "Be reconciled with God!" Then, in the part we read from the Sermon on the Mount, Jesus provides some practical how-to's: urging the traditional Jewish disciplines of almsgiving, fasting, and prayer—especially the kind that cannot be mistaken as done for show.

First Sunday of Lent

Readings: Gen 2:7-9; 3:1-7; Rom 5:12-19; Matt 4:1-11

"For just as through the disobedience of one person the many were made sinners, so through the obedience of one the many will be made righteous." (Rom 5:19)

Testing . . . One, Two, Three

The best way to see what is going on in the three-part narrative traditionally called "The Temptation of Jesus" is to read Deuteronomy 6 through 8—Moses' reflections on God's testing of Israel in the wilderness "as a man disciplines his son" (Deut 8:5). In these chapters we discover the source of all three of Jesus' responses to the devil's suggestions, in reverse order (Deut 8:3, not by bread alone; 6:16, test not God; 6:13, the Lord your God shall you worship—all responses cast in the wording of the Greek version of the Hebrew Bible). Jesus is clearly being presented as passing the tests that his ancestors failed.

As to the nature of this narrative, commentators take one of three options: (1) it is a literal record of Jesus' experience; (2) it is Jesus' summary of his struggles in the format of a dramatic rabbinic debate; (3) it is the post-Easter Church's reflection (in that dialogue format) on the significance of Jesus' public life as the reversal of Adam's and Israel's disobedience. Two considerations make option 3 the most likely: the schematic nature of the narrative, reflecting so carefully the account of Deuteronomy 6–8, and the dependence on the Greek version, which was more likely used by the post-Easter Church than by Aramaic-speaking Jesus.

When we take seriously the background of Deuteronomy 6–8, it becomes clear that the issue is Jesus' obedience as contrasted with Israel's disobedience. The tone is established early in Deuteronomy 6, where we find what eventually became Israel's central prayer, the *Shema:* "Hear, O Israel! The LORD is our God, the LORD alone. Therefore, you shall love the LORD, your God, with all your heart, and with all your soul, and with all your strength" (Deut 6:4-5). *Shema* is the Hebrew word translated "hear!", and it means not simply "attend to!" but also "respond! live it out!"—what we sometimes mean when we say, with some urgency, in American English, "Listen up!"

Notice that this episode comes right after the voice from heaven calls Jesus "my beloved Son." So this account of testing serves as a commentary on the meaning of "Son of God" as applied to Jesus. Matthew has already shown that Jesus is God's Son in the profound genetic sense as one conceived by the Holy Spirit (Matt 1:21). Moreover, the evangelist has shown Jesus to be the Son of God in a way that parallels Israel as God's son by applying to him the quotation from Hosea, "Out of Egypt I called my son" (Hos 11:1, at Matt 2:15). Notice that Matthew does not allow us to see Jesus' obedience as some kind of Christian supersession of Judaism, for Jesus does what he does as son of David and son of Abraham (Matt 1:1). So he does not supersede but rather fulfills Israel's sonship.

This Gospel reading leads inevitably to how we who worship in Jesus' name may be challenged to obedience. "Obedience" is not a popular word in pastoral discourse today, but it is essential to New Testament faith. Paul speaks of Jesus being "obedient to death" (Phil 2:8) and describes his own mission as bringing about the "obedience of faith" (Rom 1:5). Obedience (root: *ob- audire*—to hear responsively, as in *Shema!*) means more than simply carrying out orders. As in the Hebrew *Shema*, it means listening deeply and actively—to the commandments and to Church teaching, of course, but also to our conscience as we try to enact the vision of faith in our daily lives.

To cite a particular example where we U.S. Catholics exhibit a hearing difficulty, take the issue of the death penalty. For at least twenty years now, our Pope and our bishops have repeatedly expressed a developing moral doctrine of our Church, namely, that when alternatives for protecting society are available, the death penalty is always a wrongful taking of life. As in the case of abortion, though our law permits this taking of life by the state, Catholic citizens are called to say that, in our time and place, this act is simply wrong. This teaching is part of the Church's effort to forge a consistent ethic of life. At bottom, this is an effort to hear Jesus. To date, indications are that, on this topic, the majority of us have not chosen to listen up.

Second Sunday of Lent

Readings: Gen 12:1-4a; 2 Tim 1:8b-10; Matt 17:1-9

**"All the communities of the earth
shall find blessing in you." (Gen 12:3)**

ABRAM, ISRAEL, JESUS AND US

If you are a member of one of the three Abrahamic religions—that is if you are a Jew, a Christian, or a Muslim—the call of Abram (later known as Abraham) has to be one of the most powerful episodes in the Bible. If, as a matter of fact, the story is not all that important to you, you need to re-read it in context, for what comes before and after makes a world of difference.

The people who put together the book of Genesis placed this first episode of the ancestral stories right after their eleven-chapter résumé of pre-Israelite human history. Thus, when we come to chapter 12, we have read the stories of creation followed by five accounts illustrating the human capacity to violate God's intentions for creation—the rebellion of Adam and Eve, Cain's murder of Abel, the arrogance that brings on the deluge, Ham's disrespect of his father Noah, and the building of the tower of Babel. The rest of the Bible will be the story of the Creator's strategy to rescue the human part of creation from its own foolishness, through a particular people, Israel, beginning with a particular man, Abram.

Careful commentators have noticed that the call of Abram is told in a way that very consciously reverses elements of the episode that came immediately before, the tower of Babel story. Whereas the ambitious people gathered on the plain of Shinar to build their city and tower say, "Let us . . . make a great name for ourselves," childless senior Abram is told by God, "*I* will make your name great." And whereas the second goal of the builders of Babel is to prevent their being "scattered . . . all over the earth," Abram is told to abandon whatever security he had in Haran and to take the risk of going "to a land," God says, "that I will show you."

Those same careful commentators also note that the fivefold repetition of the word "bless" in this passage matches the fivefold use of "curse" in Genesis 1–11—another hint that what begins with Abram is God's strategy for undoing the damage of the whole prior history of human sinfulness.

Just how all the communities of the earth will find blessing in Abram —this is what the rest of the Bible is about. Sometimes that universal blessing is expressed in prophecies about all the nations coming to find peace and enlightenment in Zion (for example, Isaiah 2). The author of Isaiah 40–55, the one we call Second Isaiah, envisions Israel becoming a blessing for the nations as the Servant of Yahweh who is a "light for the nations" (Isa 42:6; 49:6). The Christian claim, of course, is that Jesus is the one who carries out Israel's vocation and that he continues that work through his Church (see Luke's exposition of this theme in his Gospel and in Acts). And Paul writes to the Gentile Christians of Galatia that they, too, are heirs to the promises to Abraham, since Christ is the "seed of Abraham" par excellence and they have been incorporated into Christ.

Though it may not be obvious at first, the Transfiguration vision of this Sunday's Gospel is part of that same thread stretching back to Abram. Think of what it meant for three Jews—Peter, James and John —to experience this vision. First Jesus is transfigured in a manner that anticipates his resurrection. Then he is accompanied by Moses and Elijah, who are engaged in conversation with him. If any two figures symbolize the Law and the Prophets—in effect, God's revelation to Israel—they are Moses and Elijah; and they are treating Jesus as an equal, placing him in their prophetic line as mediators of God's word and covenant. The covenant allusion comes not only from the figure of Moses but also from the bright, overshadowing cloud, reminiscent of the forging of the covenant people at Mt. Sinai. Out of that cloud, a voice proclaims that Jesus is much more than the equal of Moses and Elijah: "This is my beloved Son on whom my favor rests. Listen to him."

This, of course, is the same voice heard at the baptism of Jesus, repeating the same message. As before, the message identifies Jesus as Messiah (alluding to "You are my son," in Psalm 2:7) and the Servant of Yahweh ("in whom I am well pleased" alluding to Isaiah 42:1). That Isaian text is the first Servant song which destines the Servant to be a "light to the nations" (Isa 42:6). When the three disciples fall to the ground in fear, and are reassured by Jesus, they look and see no one but Jesus. Thus Jesus, especially as risen Lord, is the final mediator of the promise to Abram, the one through whom the Creator means to bless all the communities of the earth.

Third Sunday of Lent

Readings: Exod 17:3-7; Rom 5:1-2, 5-8; John 4:5-42

"God is Spirit, and those who worship him must worship in Spirit and truth." (John 4:24)

What We Thirst For

About ten years ago, I heard a Samaritan scholar (one of the five hundred or so Samaritans alive on planet Earth) address an audience at the local Jewish community center. I was stunned when he told those assembled, "We Samaritans and you Jews are both heirs of the ancient Israelite tradition. But the Torah says nothing about centering worship in Jerusalem. In Deuteronomy, God says to worship 'in the place where I will cause my name to dwell.' We know where that place is, Shechem, at Mount Gerizim, where Joshua first set up an altar. So we Samaritans are the authentic exponents of the Israelite tradition. You Jews are the heretics to the south." I was shocked. But the mainly Jewish audience around me did not seem disturbed. After some twenty-seven hundred years of shared history, they knew perfectly well what Samaritans thought about the right place to worship God. So they were not surprised. For me, the remark was a vivid reminder of the background that underlies part of the dialogue between Jesus and the woman at the well in this Sunday's Gospel.

The topic of Samaritans and Jews leads naturally to thoughts about what divides and what unites human beings generally. And today's Gospel story centers around what we have most in common—thirst for God. The perfect symbol for the thirst for God is our common thirst for water. Next to carbon, the thing that all life forms we know about have most in common is water. We human beings begin our early development floating in the amniotic fluid of our mother's womb. Once out of that sea-like environment, our bodies insist that we continue to imbibe water, first in our mother's milk, then wherever we can find it, all the days of our lives.

One of the best places on earth to get in touch with this human need for water is Israel and the Occupied Territories. For there fresh water sources are scarce, and the precious rainwater that falls during the winter must be captured and kept in cisterns for use during the dry part of the year. Since water held in cisterns can get stale and contaminated, people came to call the fresh water of spring-fed sources "living water," to distinguish it from the relatively "dead" water kept in cisterns. In that setting, it is easy to understand how water, especially "living water," came to be a powerful metaphor for God's relationship with human beings. Take, for example, Jeremiah's words, "Two evils have my people done: / they have forsaken me, the source of living waters; / They have dug themselves cisterns, / broken cisterns, that hold no water" (Jer 2:13). One of the tourist sites in the Holy Land with the best claim to authenticity is the well at Nablus (near ancient Shechem / Sychar). It is the only well of spring-fed water in the area, and it is likely thousands of years old.

All of this water talk helps us to follow the dialogue between Jesus and the Samaritan woman. When the Samaritan woman rebuffs Jesus' request for a drink, he says if she knew the gift of God and who was making the request, she would have asked him, and he would have given her *living water*. As so often happens in the Fourth Gospel, Jesus' interlocutor misunderstands, and takes literally ("living water" = spring-fed water) what he means figuratively ("living water" = the gift of the Holy Spirit, a meaning that is hinted here but becomes clear in John 7:37-39). (The translation "cistern" in the NAB translation of verses 11 and 12 is probably incorrect since *phrear* means simply "well," the usual rendering.)

When the woman refers to the ancient sore point between Jews and Samaritans about the right place to worship (Jerusalem or Mount Gerizim), Jesus says, "The hour is coming, and is now here, when true worshipers will worship the Father in spirit and truth. . . . God is Spirit, and those who worship him must worship in spirit and truth." This encounter prompts the woman to abandon her jar and proceed to evangelize her village, who come to believe that Jesus is "the savior of the world."

This passage speaks powerfully to our project of evangelization today. It reminds us that the Good News of God in Jesus is meant to overcome ancient hostilities and cross-cultural barriers. Though its source is concrete and specific ("salvation is from the Jews"—John 4:22), the gift of God in Jesus is meant for all who thirst for God. Jesus is the savior of the world.

Fourth Sunday of Lent

Readings: 1 Sam 16:1b, 6-7, 10-13a; Eph 5:8-14; John 9:1-41

**"For you were once darkness,
but now you are light in the Lord." (Eph 5:8)**

WE'RE ALL BLIND

We learn how to see.

We have documented cases of people who were born blind, who grew up that way, and who later on in their adult life were suddenly enabled by surgery to register optical phenomena. Surprisingly, they are not able really to see right away. Their brains do not have the skills to interpret the visual data impinging on their retinas. This experience has taught us that we have to *learn* how to see, even on the merely physical level. This is one of the first developmental tasks of a newborn baby. As infants, we gradually learn how to sort out the visual data, and with all the experimental learning that comes through baby play, we learn how to interpret the visual cues about space, distance, and how our bodies relate to the persons and objects around us. This kind of learning to see that comes naturally to a child comes as a shock to a lately sighted adult who grew up blind. This experience contributes to the drama of the film *At First Sight*. It helps us appreciate the gift of vision and the ability to use that marvelous sense.

But if we need to learn to see on the physical level, we know very well that there are still other levels of seeing that require learning. "You see what you're trained to see," I recall a sociology teacher repeating over and over. Think of what a few savvy remarks from Sister Wendy can do to your ability to see new dimensions in a familiar painting. Think how the observations of the color commentator help you realize you didn't fully see what was going on a moment ago on the tenth yardline. A physician's diagnosis lets us know that he sees something in Uncle Joe's complexion that we didn't catch.

The richness of the human experience of seeing prompts us to use that experience metaphorically to refer to understanding, as in "Do you see what I'm saying?" The same reality has led many religious writers, including our four evangelists, to use vision as a metaphor for faith. While all levels of the New Testament tradition affirm that Jesus healed persons from physical blindness, the evangelists are not content to simply relay that physical fact. They invariably tell such healings in a way that invests them with a symbolic dimension.

This Sunday's Gospel account about the man born blind is the show-case example of seeing as a symbol of believing. We know that this symbolic dimension resides in the narrative and not simply in our imagination because of the clues the author embeds in the story. For example, Jesus' statement, "I am the light of the world," calls attention to a theme already established in John's prologue when he speaks of the life of the Word as light that shines in the darkness and which the darkness has not overcome. The curious behavior of Jesus' mixing his spittle with clay and "anointing" (*epechrisen*, a verb related to *Christos*, "anointed one," or "Messiah") makes sense when John observes that the meaning of the pool's name, Siloam, is interpreted as "Sent" (or, more literally, "the Sent One" [*apestalmenos*], which serves in the Fourth Gospel as another name for Jesus).

In a community whose rite of initiation was immersion in water accompanied by anointing and was sometimes called "the enlightenment," readers and hearers of this Gospel inevitably understood this narrative not simply as a healing account but also as a meditation on the meaning of baptism and coming to faith. Baptism is surely an immersion in the water of the Sent One. In that context we are all born blind spiritually, and we do not really see the fullness of reality until we are enabled by baptism and faith to see by the light of Christ, "the light of the world." Believing is the deepest kind of seeing. Like physical vision, it is not simply a given ability; it is also something that we have to learn to use.

The reading from Ephesians speaks with the same imagery, especially if those commentators are right who claim that the passage derives from an early baptismal homily. Hear this, for example: "Awake, O sleeper, / arise from the dead, / and Christ will give you light" (Eph 5:14).

Fifth Sunday of Lent

Readings: Ezek 37:12-14; Rom 8:8-11; John 1-45

"I am the resurrection and the life; whoever believes in me, even if he dies, will live." (John 11:25)

FULLNESS OF LIFE

Who doesn't want the fullness of life? No one. Advertisers know this very well. And so they contrive commercials that prompt us to associate evocative phrases like "the fabric of our lives" or "as good as it gets" with specific products, hoping that we will associate our quest for life's fullness with the purchase of those commodities.

The Bible, of course, also makes claims about the fullness of life. It often does so in surprising language. The readings for this Sunday provide stunning examples of biblical imagery about the fullness of life.

The reading from Ezekiel—"I will open your graves and have you rise from them, and bring you back to the land of Israel"—comes as an explanation of the famous vision of the valley of the dry bones. People who do not read the whole chapter (Ezekiel 37) can miss the message entirely. Ezekiel is shown a valley full of bones and is commanded to prophesy to the bones: "See! I will bring spirit into you, that you may come to life. I will put sinews upon you, make flesh grow over you, cover you with skin, and put spirit in you so that you may come to life and know that I am the LORD." The prophet does as he is told, and in a process celebrated in the African American spiritual "Dry Bones," the bones are reconstructed into skeletons, enfleshed, and revived, "they came alive and stood upright, a vast army. Then he said to me: Son of man, these bones are the whole house of Israel. They have been saying, 'Our bones are dried up, our hope is lost, and we are cut off.'" It is at that point that today's first reading begins, with its promise to return the people to their homeland.

When we recall that Ezekiel was preaching to the Judeans living in exile in Babylon, it is clear that the passage is not first of all about resurrection. Rather, it uses resurrection imagery to describe the restoration of the people that comes about when the Persian Cyrus the Great conquers the Babylonians and allows the Judeans to return. Thus the imagery of resurrection portrays God's revival of his covenant people and the renewal of their relationship with him ("Thus you shall know that I am the LORD"). This vision proclaims that, for Israel, the fullness of their life as a people is knowing the saving power of God in that covenant relationship.

The account of the raising of Lazarus is another exploration into the fullness of life; in this case it is the fullness found by responding to Jesus as the One Sent by the Father. As is usual in the Fourth Gospel, insight comes through conversations in which there are two levels of understanding. Jesus makes statements that are misunderstood by his interlocutors because they hear him in a conventional and superficial way, whereas he means something deeper. Jesus says to his disciples that Lazarus is sleeping and that he is going to awaken him. They take the idiom of sleep and awakening literally, whereas Jesus is really talking about resuscitation of the dead man.

We soon discover that the physical resuscitation of a dead man is a sign of something deeper still. Jesus arrives four days after Lazarus's death, and Martha scolds him for not coming earlier to heal her brother. When Jesus says, "Your brother will rise," she takes this as a conventional reference to the general resurrection "on the last day." Jesus responds, "I am the resurrection and the life; whoever believes in me, even if he dies, will live, and everyone who lives and believes in me will never die." In this statement, Jesus has moved beyond the traditional Jewish expectation of the general resurrection and applied that language to the new life that a person enters by relating to him with faith.

Just as the healing of the man born blind is a sign of something else, the deeper "seeing" that is the life of faith, the raising of Lazarus from physical death is a sign of a deeper awakening to the fullness of life, the "eternal life" that comes with Christian faith. This is a variation on John 5:24—"Amen, amen, I say to you, whoever hears my word and believes in the one who sent me has eternal life and will not come to condemnation, *but has passed from death to life.*" This transformation is the fullness of life, of which the general resurrection will be a later confirmation.

Passion (Palm) Sunday

Readings: Matt 21:1-11; Isa 50:4-7; Phil 2:6-11; Matt 26:14–27:66

**"This happened so that what had been spoken through
the prophet might be fulfilled. . . ." (Matt 21:4)**

IN ACCORDANCE WITH THE SCRIPTURES

The biblical accounts of the events leading up to, and including, the death of Jesus are rich in references to the Hebrew Scriptures. Like the infancy narratives, the accounts of the passion and death of Jesus either quote directly or echo the Old Testament in almost every verse. This final week of Lent is a good time to reflect on the Christian use of the Jewish Scriptures to interpret the actions and passion of Jesus.

Over the years, it has gradually come home to me that there are two misguided ways to interpret Old Testament allusions and citations in the New Testament. The first wrong way is simply to take an Old Testament reference as a claim that a prediction came true. This bald prediction/fulfillment approach reduces the meaning of the reference to the simple thought: the Old Testament says such and such, and look, it happened in Jesus' life. Granted that this was often the way those references were treated in the apologetics of another age, this way of thinking rarely does justice to the implied intentions of the biblical authors, and these intentions vary according to context.

The other misguided way of interpreting the New Testament references to the Hebrew Scriptures is the hypothesis of some skeptical biblical critics who assume the details of the passion were simply invented by authors using the Old Testament as their source. This hardly makes sense as the practice of people proclaiming Good News.

What, then, is the best way to understand the New Testament references to the Old Testament? It is to take those references one by one, looking in each case for the way in which the older text is used to interpret the meaning of the life and person of Jesus. This Sunday's readings provide a number of fascinating examples. Let's consider two of them.

Zech 9:9 at Matt 21:5. "Behold, your king comes to you, / meek and riding on an ass, / and on a colt, the foal of a beast of burden." Mark and Luke tell of Jesus' entry into Jerusalem without quoting this explanatory verse from the prophet Zechariah. All of the Synoptic Gospels are clear that Jesus' choice of the donkey as his mount for entering Jerusalem was quite deliberate. The move is so carefully prearranged that one suspects that it is some kind of prophetic symbolic action—like the table fellowship with outcasts or the sharing of the cup of blessing. Matthew makes the meaning of the choice evident by citing Zechariah 9:9, which is part of a portrait of a future king who rides a donkey instead of a war horse, a peacemaking king who bans the bow and the chariot. (The Fourth Gospel will clarify the meaning even further, not only by quoting the prophet but also by showing Jesus choosing to ride the donkey *in response to* the palm-waving of the crowds.) Notice that the citation of Zechariah is more than a matter of highlighting a fulfilled prediction; it explains the meaning of the action.

Wis 2:16-18 at Matt 27:43. To Mark's description of the passers-by and the chief priests and scribes taunting the crucified Jesus to save himself and come down from the cross, Matthew adds some words. "Let him come down from the cross now, and we will belive in him," say the passers-by. And the Temple officials add the barb, "He trusted in God; let him deliver him now if he wants him. For he said, 'I am the Son of God.'" This Matthean addition is a paraphrase of Wisdom 2:17-18, whose context is a description of a group of wicked men who think that might makes right (Wis 2:11) ganging up on a just man and speaking cynically among themselves: "He boasts that God is his Father. / Let us see whether his words are true . . . For if the just one be the son of God, he will defend him / and deliver him from the hand of his foes . . ." (Wis 2:16-18). This allusion to the Old Testament is clearly not a matter of prediction and fulfillment. For the author of Wisdom, it is a perennial scenario. As applied to Jesus, the reference is a reflection on the meaning of the drama that Jesus plays out; for the Wisdom passage also comments on the delusion of the abusers of the just man: "These were their thoughts, but they erred; / for their wickedness blinded them, / And they knew not the hidden counsels God, / neither did they count on a recompense of holiness, / nor discern the innocent souls' reward. . . ." (Wis 2:21-22). Thus Matthew enlists the Wisdom text not as prediction but as illumination.

These examples are just a taste of the wealth of meaning that lies behind the echoes of Scripture in the passion account.

Easter Vigil (Resurrection of the Lord)

Readings: Gen 1:1–2:2; Gen 22:1-18; Exod 14:15–15:1;
Isa 54:5-14; Isa 55:1-11; Bar 3:9-15, 32–4:4; Ezek 36:16-28;
Rom 6:3-11; Matt 28:1-10

> **"We were indeed buried with him through baptism**
> **into death, so that, just as Christ was raised**
> **from the dead by the glory of the Father,**
> **we too might live in newness of life." (Rom 6:4)**

ALL THOSE VIGIL READINGS

The center of gravity in the liturgical celebration of Easter is the Vigil. In the darkness of night, we begin a celebration that launches the seven Sundays of Easter (note, not seven Sundays *after* Easter). Since nine readings are assigned for the Easter Vigil, eight of them followed by responsorial psalms, we do well to prepare for that celebration by reflecting on how that rich anthology hangs together.

Gen 1:1–2:2.—We hear this reading right after dispersing the darkness with the Easter fire, the lighting of the paschal candle and the proclamation of Christ as the light of the world. However we understand the origin and development of the cosmos scientifically, the poetry of Genesis 1 expresses powerfully our faith that it is the God of Israel who ordered chaos, brought light into darkness, introduced life into an inanimate cosmos, and made a watery planet humanly habitable. That same Creator finally introduced the eternal Word made flesh as the ultimate light of the world to address the darkness of human sinfulness. Fire and water come into play in the sacrament that celebrates our participation in that victory.

Gen 22:1-18.—The promise that Abraham will become the ancestor of a great people who will be a blessing to all the nations—that promise rides on Isaac, and Abraham is asked by the Promisor to sacrifice his only son. This classic and scandalous account speaks to our celebration in at least two ways. Abraham's readiness to let go of everything mirrors the divine outpouring manifested in the life, death, and resurrection of Jesus ("God so loved the world that he gave his only Son . . ."). It also foreshadows the paradox at the heart of Jesus' teaching: Whoever loses his life for my sake and that of the Gospel, will save it.

Exod 14:15–15:1.—This account of the liberation of Israel from slavery through the sea is the key narrative of Israel's experience of divine redemption. The biblical authors describe the moment as a new creation. As in Genesis 1, the God of wind and water orders chaos by separating water in making dry land. In this, God is victorious over that violator of created order, the Pharaoh. Thus early Christian writers, and we, use this narrative to reflect on the new creation of baptism.

Isa 54:5-14.—This passage from Second Isaiah was first preached to the Judean exiles in Babylon. The prophet proclaims the end of exile and return to the homeland as a renewal of the covenant of peace renewed with Noah after the flood (Genesis 9). The end of exile is such a fresh start that the prophet can speak of it as a new creation. For us gathered around the light of Christ, baptism into the body of Christ is also an end to exile, a renewal of creation.

Isa 55:1-11.—The exiles were invited to a conversion that would lead to participation in the covenant promised to David and to a leadership role among the nations. Similarly, our baptism was a covenant renewal, not only for our benefit but for the sake of the rest of the world. Our renewal calls us to share in Jesus' Jewish mission to be a light to the nations.

Bar 3:9-15, 32; 4:4.—A second-century B.C.E. author writing in the person of Jeremiah's secretary, Baruch, makes a parallel between his situation and that of the exiles some four centuries earlier: the people are still in a kind of spiritual exile and need to attend to God's wisdom expressed in the Torah. Christians have long applied these words to our situation. For us, Wisdom "has appeared on earth and moved among people" in Jesus.

Ezek 36:16-28.—Here another exilic prophet speaks of God's plan to restore and renew Israel. The language of cleansing with water and giving a new heart and a new spirit was ready-made for Christian application to the new life found in the body of Christ.

Rom 6:3-11.—Paul's reflection on baptism as dying and rising to new life names the event to which all the readings have been pointing.

Matt 28:1-10.—Matthew's account of the women's discovery of the empty tomb and their commissioning by the risen Lord sounds the full note of Easter joy, peace, and mission that captures for us the new thing that the Creator has been doing for the past two millennia.

Easter Sunday

Readings: Acts 10:34, 37-43; Col 3:1-4 (or 1 Cor 5:6-8); John 20:1-9

**"They put him to death by hanging him on a tree.
This man God raised [on] the third day and
granted that he be visible, not to all the people,
but to us, the witnesses chosen by God in advance,
who ate and drank with him after he rose from the dead."
(Acts 10:39-41)**

The Age to Come Is Here

Whatever Jesus had said to his followers about his death and resurrection—they were simply not prepared for either reality. Mark says that most of them scattered after the arrest and were not around for the crucifixion. John notes that they were cowering behind locked doors on what turned out to be Easter Sunday. And this Sunday's Gospel, John's account of the discovery of the empty tomb, shows Mary Magdalene, and then Peter and the beloved disciple, as initially clueless. For Magdalene, the discovery that the stone had been rolled back could mean only one thing: grave robbers; someone had carried off the body of her Master. When she informs Peter and the beloved disciple, they run to the tomb to verify her report. On closer inspection they notice not just the absence of the body; they notice the linen wrapping lying on the ground, and the napkin that had bound Jesus' face set aside and nicely rolled up. What to make of this? Would grave robbers have bothered to undress the corpse before carrying it off? And would not the removal of linen bonded to a bloody body be a difficult and uninviting task? And is not the whole point of grave robbery to loot treasure? Of what commercial value is a corpse? No. The presence of the wrapping demanded another explanation.

Most people are aware that the famous Shroud of Turin has long been venerated as precisely the wrappings mentioned in John's account.

While the jury is still out regarding the authenticity of the Shroud, some of the observations of its scientific analyzers raise some fascinating questions about that piece of cloth. Trying to account for the negative image scorched on the linen and the nature of the blood stains, one (non-Christian) examiner said, in effect, "The only way I can account for these phenomena is that, to leave the blood stains intact and to produce this kind of image, the body must have somehow *passed through* the cloth."

We'd love to know more about what exactly transpired in that tomb. On one point, though, the New Testament accounts are insistent: resurrection is not resuscitation. When St. Paul takes up that issue with the Christian community of Corinth, he makes it clear that the risen body is not a mere return to biological existence. Nor is resurrection an entirely nonphysical existence with no continuity with the premortem body. It is a bodily existence all right, but a bodily existence that has been transformed. Paul uses the analogy of the seed that is planted, and the vegetation that emerges. The seed has been transformed into a new existence (1 Cor 15:36-38).

Well, however such considerations fascinate our late-twentieth-century minds, they are not the aspects of Jesus' resurrection that fired up his Jewish followers. For them, Jesus' resurrection was not just about the body of one person. His resurrection was about world history. Yes, world history. In first-century Palestine, there were several ways of thinking about postmortem existence. The Sadducees didn't believe in any kind of life after death. The Pharisees, however, did. They developed the teaching of the book of Daniel into an understanding that a general resurrection of the faithful in Israel would be part of the "age to come"—the time when the kingdom of God would be manifest by the restoration of the tribes of Israel, the outpouring of the Holy Spirit, and the establishment of peace and justice. For people who thought this way—and Jesus and his followers apparently did—resurrection from the dead was part of the larger package of this Age to Come.

Once they experienced Jesus as their risen Lord, present to some of them in very bodily ways—the last one being Paul's own privileged experience on the road to Damascus—there was one obvious conclusion. If Jesus had been raised from the dead, then the Age to Come—the kingdom of God—must have arrived! That's why the New Testament writers use the bold language of new creation to describe Christian existence.

The resurrection is not simply a proof that Jesus is truly son of God; it is also the sign that cosmic history has taken a new and fresh turn. We can sense this in the reading from Colossians 3. Paul dares to tell the Christians of Colossae that they have already died and been raised up with Christ. That is his way of reminding them that their baptism has begun a new kind of existence for them in this Age to Come. When he goes on to urge them to "think of what is above, not of what is on earth," it sounds like he is urging a kind of withdrawal from ordinary life. As we read on in this letter, however, it becomes clear that he is very much thinking of ordinary life. He says that the negative stuff we all deal with—anger, lust, greed, deception—must be addressed with the healing power of the new life we have in Christ. The resurrection of Jesus enables us to let God reign in our ordinary lives in ways that demonstrate we are part of a new creation—not complete, obviously (just think of ethnic cleansing), but that kingdom is evident wherever communities allow the spirit of the risen Lord to have its way.

Second Sunday of Easter

Readings: Acts 2:42-47; 1 Pet 1:3-9; John 20:19-31

**"Blessed are those who have not seen
and have believed." (John 20:29)**

BEING SAVED

Faith in the resurrection of Jesus Christ is much more than simply believing in an amazing fact. Each of this Sunday's readings reminds us that belief in Jesus' resurrection is accepting and participating in a relationship that can enliven every part of our lives—now and forever.

John may speak of Jesus appearing simply to "the disciples," unnumbered and unnamed, to help us later readers include ourselves in the picture. To enable those disciples to be sent as Jesus was sent, Jesus breathes on them and says, "Receive the holy Spirit." When we recall that this remarkable action is occurring near the end of a book that began with the words, "In the beginning," it is not hard to see in this breathing an allusion to the creation of Adam. Easter enables a new creation: a frightened people are empowered to live out Jesus' mission of sharing the life of God with others through their own self-giving in imitation of Jesus. If the beatitude, "Blessed are those who have not seen and have believed," is not clear enough for us, the author's own statement of purpose is crystal clear: "These [signs] are written that you may [come to] believe that Jesus is the Messiah, the Son of God, and that through this belief you may have life in his name" (John 20:31).

If we want a concrete illustration of what "life in his name" entails, we need look no further than the cameo picture that Luke provides in today's first reading from Acts. Although vowed religious communities have, through the centuries, taken this summary as a model for their community life, the context of this passage in Acts suggests that Luke intends this to be a portrait of Christian community generally. The details are worth pondering.

They devoted themselves to the teaching [didachē] *of the apostles, to the communal life* [koinōnia], *to the breaking of the bread and to the prayers.* We recognize here the perennial ingredients of Church life. The apostolic "teaching" would, no doubt, include the sayings of Jesus and the interpretations of his life by way of texts from the Hebrew Scriptures. The "communal life" includes the generous sharing of possessions mentioned later in this description. The "breaking of the bread" seems to be, as in the Emmaus account in Luke's Gospel (Luke 24), the celebration of the Lord's Supper. And "the prayers" likely include continued engagement in the Temple liturgy.

Awe [phobos] *came upon everyone.* Some translations interpret this as a description of outsiders' response to the apostolic "wonders and signs," but the statement can just as easily be taken as a description of the community itself. If so, it likely refers to that fear of God which the Hebrew Scriptures name as the beginning of wisdom. Belief in the resurrection of Jesus, repentance, baptism, and the gift of the Holy Spirit (Acts 2:38-41) have revived in these pious Jews an awe for the presence and power of the Creator.

And many wonders and signs were done through the apostles. "Wonders and signs" (with its peculiar reversal of the usual order "signs and wonders") echoes the wonders and signs mentioned in the quotation from Joel and applied to Jesus' healing actions in Peter's Pentecost speech (2:19, 22). By using the same phrase here, Luke underscores the fact that the apostles continue the divinely empowered ministry of Jesus (soon to be illustrated by the healing of the lame man through Peter and John [Acts 3]).

All who believed were together and had all things in common; they would sell their property and possessions and divide them among all according to each one's need. This spells out part of what is meant by the earlier mention of communal life. The very phrasing suggests that such sharing of goods is a spontaneous expression of the Easter faith. When one takes the Creator personally, one uses creatures differently and more generously.

Every day they devoted themselves to meeting together in the temple area and to breaking bread in their homes. This note puts us in touch with the realities that the Jerusalem Christian community still saw themselves as Jews very much in contact with their Israelite tradition and community, and that their own homes served as the place for the Christian breaking of the bread. Strikingly, Luke can use the descriptive word *sōzomenoi*—"those who were being saved"—to describe new Christians.

Third Sunday of Easter

Readings: Acts 2:14, 22-33; 1 Pet 1:17-21; Luke 24:13-35

> **"But God raised him up, releasing him from the throes of death, because it was impossible for him to be held by it." (Acts 2:24)**

> **". . . realizing that you were ransomed from your futile conduct, handed on by your ancestors . . . ." (1 Pet 1:18)**

> **"But we were hoping that he would be the one to redeem Israel . . . ." (Luke 24:21)**

EASTER'S FREEDOM

Redemption is one of those biblical words with a powerful, but largely forgotten, image at its root. It comes from a Latin word meaning literally "buying back"—as in the liberation of a slave by ransom. So to be redeemed means to be freed from slavery. Unfortunately, some theologians, over the centuries, got distracted by the literal image of buying back and asked, in the case of Christian redemption, to *whom* the payment was made. This led to theories about Satan somehow getting paid off. The point of the word redemption, of course, is the essential metaphor of release from bondage, not the commercial transaction by which such release sometimes occurs in society.

On this third Sunday of Easter, it is worth noting that each of the three readings speaks of the resurrection of Jesus and its consequences in terms of release from bondage.

First, we hear a section of Peter's speech at Pentecost (the first sentence, followed by the middle third of the speech). We hear Peter (or Luke the speech writer working with second-generation hindsight) applying Hebrew Scripture to the experience of the resurrection. Earlier, the speech interpreted the prophetic utterances of the Spirit-filled community as realizations of Joel's prophecy about end-time "wonders and signs" and the pouring out of God's spirit upon all flesh. Now, in this part, the speaker announces that the mighty works Jesus did were already end-time wonders and signs worked by God.

Then Peter proceeds to show how Scripture also helps us understand Jesus' resurrection. He observes that Psalm 16 (attributed to David, as all of the psalms were in those days) uses words that really make no sense as applied to David. For David says in the psalm, "Nor will you suffer your faithful one to undergo corruption." Well, says Peter, we have to acknowledge that David's body did indeed suffer corruption; it had been moldering in its Jerusalem grave for a good thousand years. The words of the psalm find their fitting application in Jesus. As the remainder of the speech spells out, "Since [David] was a prophet and knew that God had sworn an oath to him that he would set one of his descendants upon his throne, he foresaw and spoke of the resurrection of the Messiah, that neither was *he* abandoned to the netherworld nor did *his* flesh see corruption" (Acts 2:30-31).

We are so accustomed to thinking of Jesus rising from death on his own power that we forget something: the usual New Testament language about the resurrection is that *God* raised Jesus from the dead. In other words, the resurrection is not simply an act of the Son; it is a trinitarian affair, with the Father raising the Son in the power of the Spirit.

This way of speaking of the resurrection (and our participation in it) as a liberating act of the Trinity is also reflected in the reading from 1 Peter. The author reminds recently converted Gentiles scattered among the Roman provinces of Asia Minor that they have been delivered from the futile way of their ancestors by the Blood of the Lamb. Here the liberation image is linked to its roots in the redemption from slavery in Exodus. Christians are involved in a new Exodus.

Finally, freedom talk surfaces in an ironic way in today's Gospel. The forlorn disciples say to the risen, but still unrecognized, Jesus: "We were hoping that he was the one who would set Israel free." They thought that the recent death by crucifixion of their master had signaled the end of that hope. They were not impressed by the news of the empty tomb and the women's talk about a vision of angels declaring Jesus alive. Were these disciples wrong to hope for a political liberation of Israel? Not really. For Israel's hopes for "the Age to Come" entailed the restoration of the twelve tribes of Israel and the freedom from foreign empires that they had enjoyed under David. It will take a lot of post-Easter reflection and the grace of Pentecost for them to recognize that these hopes for restoration and freedom are fulfilled in the kingdom of God now guided by the spirit of the risen Lord, although he reigns in a very different way than they had expected.

Fourth Sunday of Easter

Readings: Acts 2:14a, 36-41; 1 Pet 2:20b-25; John 10:1-10

**"For the promise is made to you and
to your children and to all those far off,
whomever the Lord our God will call." (Acts 2:39)**

The House of Israel and Those Far Off

As the Church began to flourish and spread after that first Easter, the main tool it had to proclaim its Good News to the rest of the world was the language of the Hebrew Scriptures. More often than not, the version they used was the Greek one. That detail may sound like something that ought to be reserved to the footnotes of scholarly tomes. In fact, it sometimes makes a considerable difference in our understanding of the New Testament. The little speeches that make up about a third of the Acts of the Apostles provide abundant examples of Christian use of the Hebrew Scriptures in Greek.

This Sunday's first reading gives us the end of Peter's Pentecost speech, along with its immediate aftermath. When Peter refers to his audience (Jews gathered in from a worldwide Diaspora) as "the whole house of Israel," he is using a term that implies that his listeners constitute potentially the "restored Israel" of "the age to come." For, earlier in the same speech, Peter had cited Joel 3, understanding that passage as relating to "the last days," and interpreting those last days as what was beginning to happen then and there on that particular Pentecost.

That same passage from Joel also said, "And it shall be that everyone shall be saved / who *calls on the name of the Lord*" (Acts 2:21). In Joel's context, that statement referred to those who cast themselves on the mercy of Yahweh. In the language of Acts, "the Lord" is understood as a title for Jesus, and so "those who call upon the name of the Lord" becomes virtually a name for all Christians (see Acts 9:14, 21; 22:16). It is with that meaning that Peter invites his audience to be baptized in the name of Jesus Christ. In so doing, they too will receive the gift of the Holy Spirit prophesied in that same Joel passage.

Just after that last line quoted from Joel, there is a further statement, which in its Greek version says, "In Mount Zion and in Jerusalem *there will be a remnant,* just as the Lord said, and *they will be preached the good news,* those whom the Lord summons." When we read this, the aptness of the Joel passage becomes even more obvious, for it speaks not only of the outpouring of the Spirit of God but also of the preaching of Good News to a remnant of Israel in Jerusalem.

Then Peter's speech reaches out to the rest of the human family: "For the promise is made to you and to your children and to all those far off, whomever the Lord our God will call." "The promise" is the one made to Abraham: "In your descendants all the nations of the earth shall find blessing" (Gen 22:18). Like Paul in Galatians 3:6-9, Luke understands that this promise was fulfilled especially in the gift of the Holy Spirit to Gentiles as well as Jews. And the inclusion of Gentiles comes through as well in the phrase "those far off," which in the Greek version of Isaiah 57:19 appears to refer to the Gentiles. Thus a single stunning passage in the Hebrew Scriptures (even more strongly in the Greek version) supplies an explanation of both their own revitalized life and the Church's mandate for mission.

Our second reading, from 1 Peter, interprets the fourth Servant Song of Isaiah (52:13–53:12). Here, the author takes a passage that Jews understood (and still understand) as portraying Israel as a witness to the nations, and he applies it to Jesus (fulfilling Israel's role).

The Gospel passage has for its background a number of Old Testament passages about God and God's Anointed One imaged as shepherds, especially Ezekiel 34. In this vision, the prophet excoriates the "shepherds" of Israel who "pastured themselves" and failed to heal the sick or seek the lost (Ezek 34:4). He quotes God saying, "I myself will pasture my sheep." Further, God will do this through an agent: "I will appoint one shepherd over them to pasture them, my servant David" (34:23).

The previous chapter of John had shown Jesus doing the work of the Good Shepherd, healing the man born lame and then "seeking him out" later—all this despite the abuse of those "bad shepherds," the religious officials, who are portrayed as blind in their arrogance. In this Sunday's Gospel, Jesus describes himself as the Good Shepherd who leads his sheep to fullness of life.

The more seriously we take the Jewish sources of our Christian language, the better we understand that language and the more we recognize that we are the "far off" ones who have been extended the hospitality of the house of Israel by its shepherd.

Fifth Sunday of Easter

Readings: Acts 6:1-7; 1 Pet 2:4-9; John 14:1-12

> **"But you are 'a chosen race, a royal priesthood,**
> **a holy nation, a people of his own.'" (1 Pet 2:9)**

SNAPSHOTS OF A GROWING CHURCH

When Luke sketches scenes from the story of the early days of the Church in Jerusalem, he is not simply recording events. He is providing paradigms that portray something about the Church's nature. And the scenario we meet today in the first reading is not entirely a pretty picture.

"At that time, as the number of disciples continued to grow, the Hellenists complained against the Hebrews because their widows were being neglected in the daily distribution *[diakonia]*" (6:1). The "Hellenists" are best understood as Greek-speaking Jews (probably people who grew up in the Diaspora and later emigrated to Judea). "Hebrews," then, would be Aramaic-speaking Jews. We have evidence, even as far back as the Maccabees, that there had long been tension between the Jews who had taken on the language and even some of the ways of the Hellenistic world, on the one hand, and the more traditional Jews who preferred to speak Aramaic, on the other. The passage from Acts 6 lets us know that the infant Christian community of Jerusalem included Jews from both subgroups, and that becoming Christian did not automatically erase the "liberal/conservative" baggage that they brought with them. Luke informs us that the community had set up a daily distribution (of food?) to take care of the needy among them, especially widows. But the Greek-speaking widows were somehow being neglected.

Where did that neglect come from? A combination of scarcity and prejudice? Were the ("Hebrew") Twelve favoring their own kind? Were they too busy to oversee the distribution properly? Whatever the cause of the neglect, the Twelve chose to apply a familiar practical solution:

51

they increased the staff. Too busy with the *diakonia* of the word to tie up their time with serving at table (or, in another valid translation, "keeping accounts"), they call the entire community together and mandate it to select seven good men to carry out this other *diakonia*. That the seven chosen all have Greek names suggests a kind of affirmative action on the part of the community: they chose Greek-speaking members, thereby assuring that the neglect of Hellenist widows would be remedied. This freeing up of the apostles led to continuing rapid growth of the Church, even attracting some of the Temple priests to the fold.

This vignette shows the Spirit-filled community facing a very human set of problems and acting practically and faithfully. The second reading, from what appears to be a baptismal homily embedded in 1 Peter, describes the Church in a very different way. It is a densely layered poem made of imagery mined from the Law, the Prophets, and the Psalms.

Urging the recently baptized, whom he calls "born again," the writer/homilist invites them to "come to [the Lord], a living stone, rejected by human beings but chosen and precious in the sight of God." The author here draws upon an application to Jesus of Psalm 118:22 attributed both to Jesus himself (Luke 20:18) and to Peter (Acts 4:11). The original meaning of the psalm was to call Israel a stone rejected by the mighty empires around it but nonetheless destined to become a foundation stone in God's own victorious work. Such is now true of Jesus, the rejected stone now becomes the foundation stone of the "spiritual house," the Church. The baptized person is encouraged to participate in the victory of his resurrection. Preparing to describe the community as temple, he calls Jesus a "living" stone to highlight the reality that the Church is no inanimate object but a living unity, in which the new Christian is a living stone.

Shifting the image slightly, but remaining in the Temple ambiance, the author reminds the baptized that they, collectively, are to grow into "a holy priesthood to offer spiritual sacrifices acceptable to God through Jesus Christ." Like Paul in Romans 12:1-2, Peter makes it clear that by "spiritual sacrifices" he means the basic relationships of community life: "Since you have purified yourselves by obedience to the truth for sincere mutual love, love one another intensely from a [pure] heart" (1 Pet 1:22). The author ends the poem by applying to the Church phrases used in Exodus 19:5-6 to describe the covenant community of Israel at Sinai: "a royal priesthood, a holy nation, a people of his own."

Luke the historian describes the Church facing a knotty administrative challenge. Peter describes the same Church in a poem that plays Hebrew refrains in a new key. Both picture the Church, ever human, always guided by a power greater than itself.

Sixth Sunday of Easter

Readings: Acts 8:5-8, 14-17; 1 Pet 3:15-18; John 14:15-21

> **". . . they sent them [the Samaritans] Peter and John,
> who went down and prayed for them,
> that they might receive the holy Spirit, for it had not
> yet fallen upon any of them." (Acts 8:14-16)**

BAPTISM IN THE SPIRIT

"Have you been baptized in the Spirit?" Beginning some thirty years ago, exponents of the prayer movement known first as the Pentecostal movement (later, as the charismatic renewal) posed this question to their uninitiated friends. Most of us probably answered with something like, "I thought I received the Holy Spirit when I was baptized." "No," the questioner continued. "I'm talking about receiving a further in-filling of the Spirit that comes when you let a group pray with you for that gift. It can change your life."

What often followed was testimony about the adult conversion experience that such group prayer often occasioned for people who participated in the charismatic prayer groups that began to spread among the mainline Christian churches in the late 60s and early 70s. Members of such groups began to speak of their friends and their priests as either "Spirit-filled" or not, and a new insider/outsider language began to be heard among the churches.

The source of the confusion came from the vocabulary of the Assemblies of God, where the contemporary charismatic movement took its origin. They distinguish between water baptism and spirit baptism. And they use this Sunday's first reading to substantiate this distinction. On the face of it, the passage does seem to support their claim. For the text says plainly that the Samaritans "had only been baptized in the name of the Lord Jesus" and that it took the special and later prayer of Peter and John for them to receive the Holy Spirit.

53

But in another passage, Luke tells of these events happening in the opposite order. When Peter preaches to the household of Cornelius (Acts 10), Luke says that "the holy Spirit fell upon all who were listening to the word." The Jewish Christians who accompanied Peter were astounded that the gift of the holy Spirit should have been poured out on the Gentiles also. Peter observes, "Can anyone withhold the water for baptizing these people, who have received the holy Spirit even as we have."

Does Luke intend in these narratives to teach a distinction between spirit baptism and water baptism? Luke seems to provide the norm for understanding the link between baptism and the gift of the Spirit in Peter's speech on Pentecost. On that occasion Peter says, "Repent and be baptized, every one of you, in the name of Jesus Christ for the forgiveness of your sins, and you will receive the gift of the holy Spirit" (Acts 2:38).

The Gospel language about "baptizing in the Spirit" derives from the preaching of John the Baptist. Clearly, the Baptist makes a distinction between his prophetic (and pre-Christian) water baptism and the baptism in the Spirit that will come with Jesus (see Luke 3:16). And the rest of Luke–Acts makes it clear that the language normally refers to the Christian conversion-initiation experience of people receiving the Holy Spirit on the occasion of their baptism. The apparent exceptions can be accounted for by Luke's purposes. In the case of Peter and John laying hands on the Samaritans, the point is that the Samaritan mission (the first mission beyond Judaism) receives apostolic approval. And in the case of Peter with the Cornelius household, the point is that the movement of the Christian mission to the Gentiles has been divinely initiated.

In the biblical sense of getting baptized in the Spirit, then, every baptized Christian is baptized in the Spirit. What the charismatic renewal has highlighted is the genuine truth that sometimes adults do need to pray in community to let that gift of the Holy Spirit become more manifest in their lives. Understood within that framework, the readings for the Sixth Sunday of Easter (and for Ascension as well) give us rich texts to illustrate what life in the Spirit means. It means being ready to respond to those who ask the reason "for your hope" (1 Pet 3:15). It means discovering that our obedience to Jesus' teaching enables us to know the Holy Spirit as our Advocate (John 14:15-21). It means letting ourselves be called from apocalyptic sky-gazing and allowing the power of the Spirit to spur us on to mission in the world around us.

Seventh Sunday of Easter

Readings: Acts 1:12-14; 1 Pet 4:13-16; John 17:1-11a

**"Now this is eternal life, that they should know you,
the only true God, and the one whom you sent,
Jesus Christ." (John 17:3)**

BETWEEN ASCENSION AND PENTECOST

This Sunday rounds out the seven Sundays of Easter, the season of the Church's explicit celebration of the resurrection and its meaning for Christian life. At the same time, this seventh Sunday, coming between Ascension Thursday and Pentecost Sunday, focuses exquisitely on the transition between the departure of Jesus' physical presence to his followers and the birth of the Church with the end-time outpouring of the Holy Spirit. Granted that we later generations of Christians live in an era long after Pentecost, there is something about this transitional moment, which Luke symbolizes as a ten-day segue, that can help us understand our own moment in salvation history.

Today's first reading gives us Luke's snapshot of the apostles and other disciples gathered in prayer in that interval of time. While they were still gaping at the sky after the ascension, angels sent them back into the rest of history with a jibe: "Men of Galilee, why are you standing there looking at the sky?"

Instinctively, they gather with the rest of the little band of disciples in the upper room, where some of them had shared the Last Supper with their master. Luke will note that they number about 120. This numeric note is more than mere census; the multiple of twelve underscores Luke's conviction that this Jerusalem community of "Jews for Jesus" begins to fulfill the ancient expectation that "The Age to Come" would entail the restoration of Israel. The list of eleven disciples is conspicuous for the absence of Judas. The first agenda item for this post-ascension community will be the restoration of the core group to the number twelve, showing the apostolic concern for restoring the number to the very meaning of Jesus' original choice of a symbolic Twelve. The mention of "Mary the mother of Jesus" recalls the only other times Luke refers to Jesus' mother by name, the accounts of the conception (1:27) and the birth (2:5) of Jesus. The mention of her by name here in Acts underscores the fact that a new birth in the power of the Spirit is about to occur, the birth of the Church on Pentecost. Like Jesus praying after the baptism at the Jordan River, just before a fresh manifestation of the Holy Spirit in his life, the 120 in the upper room "devoted themselves with one accord to prayer" (1:14).

Though we live long after Pentecost, Luke's scenario reminds us of some perennial realities about being Church. Though life in the community of faith requires plenty of nitty-gritty administrative tasks (like electing a replacement for Judas), at the end of the day, the Church takes its life from an act of God. Like the birth of Jesus itself, the Church is conceived and brought to birth by the Holy Spirit. As in its inception, the continued life of the Church demands ongoing communal prayer and openness to the Spirit, never forgetting that we always pray with Mary.

In this Sunday's Gospel, John addresses many of these same post-Easter realities couched in much different language in the prayer of Jesus concluding his Last Supper farewell discourses. As in Acts 1, the focus of John 17 is on the transition between the earthly ministry of Jesus and the life of the post-Easter Church.

To modern ears not attuned to the biblical roots of the New Testament writing, talk of "glory" can carry vague and sentimental associations. But for people of John's and Jesus' time and place, glory meant the visible manifestation of God's presence and power. We first meet this meaning of "glory" in John's prologue: "And the Word became flesh / and made his dwelling among us, / and we saw his glory, / the glory as of the Father's only Son, / full of grace and truth" (1:14). The incarnation of the eternal and creative Word in Jesus is the manifestation of the presence of God in the humanity of Jesus. Here in the prayer of John 17, Jesus refers to his public life as an expression of the glory of the Son's own pre-creation presence to the Father. Toward the end of the part quoted as today's Gospel, he says that he has been glorified in his disciples. This way of thinking led to our insight that the purpose of the Church is to be the primary sacrament of the incarnation. This sense of "glory" helps us understand Jesus' prayer at the end of John 17, where he says, "I have given them the glory you gave me, so that they may be one, as we are one, I in them and you in me, that they may be brought to perfection as one, that the world may know that you sent me, and that you loved them even as you loved me" (17:22-23).

Pentecost Sunday

Readings: Acts 2:1-11; 1 Cor 12:3b-7, 12-13; John 20:19-21

"On the evening of that first day of the week, when the doors were locked, where the disciples were, for fear of the Jews, Jesus came and stood in their midst . . ."
(John 20:19)

RUNAWAYS BLESSED AND MISSIONED

Resurrection, the outpouring of the Holy Spirit, mission—whereas Luke spreads these events across fifty days in Luke–Acts, the Fourth Gospel concentrates them into the scenario of a single day. This is one of the places that frustrates the historical literalists who insist on finding answers to the question—exactly what happened, precisely when and where? The texts of Luke–Acts and John do not yield answers to that kind of questioning. What these texts do assert is that soon after the death and resurrection of Jesus, God, beginning in Jerusalem, presented Jesus live to a stunned and frightened group of Jesus' disciples and proceeded to enable them by the power of the Holy Spirit to continue Jesus' mission.

The fact that our New Testament canon includes more than one way of telling about this demonstrates that the Church lives easily with the fact that there is almost always more than one way to speak of the Trinity's action in Jesus. Our business is to attend carefully to what each diverse account contributes to our understanding of the essential mystery of God's action in the world.

John sets the scene in a startling way: "On the evening of that first day of the week, when the doors were locked, where the disciples were, for fear of the Jews, Jesus came and stood in their midst and said to them, 'Peace be with you.'" Clearly, whatever Jesus may have said about his imminent death and resurrection, the disciples were entirely unprepared for the shock of his execution. Their first concern after learning of their Master's death by Roman crucifixion, apparently, was for their own safety. If the Romans considered Jesus dangerous enough to kill, surely they, the followers, might be next. John's phrase "for fear of the Jews" has, or ought to have, a strange sound for our ears. After all, they themselves were Jews, as was Jesus himself. The fact is, the Fourth Gospel frequently calls Jesus' adversaries (especially the religious officials of his day) "the Jews." One can only make sense of this nomenclature by postulating that, at the time of the writing of the Fourth Gospel, the Christian community was largely Gentile and "the Jews" was for them a way of naming their own opponents. Then it becomes a way to name Jesus' opponents during his own earthly ministry. (Were John with us today, and given the sad history of Christian anti-Semitism, one suspects that he would delete the phrase "the Jews" as failing to communicate what he had intended.)

Jesus' first statement to these frightened (and no doubt guilt-ridden) runaways is, "Peace be with you." Before they have a chance to express regret and ask for forgiveness, Jesus blesses them with *shalom*. Then, to confirm his identity, Jesus shows them the wounds of his hands and side. He follows this with another blessing of *shalom*, this time linked with the mandate to carry on his mission: "As the Father has sent me, so I send you." Given all that this Fourth Gospel has said about Jesus as "sent" by the Father—to be light for the world, to heal, to be bread from heaven, to be good shepherds, to die in order to gather into one the scattered children of God, to be the New Temple, to be the culmination of divine presence in human history—to be sent by the Father *as Jesus was sent* is a thought that requires the use of a phrase from the vocabulary of today's youth—totally awesome.

If that way of describing the disciples' mission is breathtaking, it is also breath-*giving*. For Jesus implements the commission with a powerful and resonant gesture: he breathes upon them. An action that demands an explanation—breathing upon an entire group is surely an attention-getting gesture—this is another of Jesus' prophetic symbolic actions, like his washing of feet at the Last Supper. The key to the gesture's meaning is the only other scene in the Bible that even comes close, the creation of Adam (Gen 2:7), where God is pictured as breathing life into a clay model. Thus the post-Easter gift of the Holy Spirit upon the disciples comes in the form of a new creation entailing a mission that implements the very mission of the original Sent One.

Now it becomes clear why John, in his account of the healing of the man born blind, highlights the name of the pool of healing water (Siloam, meaning "the Sent One"). All of us are born blind, until we wash in the waters of the Sent One, baptized into the life of faith. Like the healed blind man, our destiny is simply to witness with our lives how we have been healed of fear and blindness and empowered to continue Jesus' mission.

Holy Trinity

Readings: Exod 34:3-6, 8-9; 2 Cor 13:11-13; John 3:16-18

**"For God so loved the world that he gave his only Son,
so that everyone who believes in him might not perish
but might have eternal life." (John 3:16)**

LIVING TRINITY

For many, approaching Trinity Sunday as the Sunday after Pentecost is both logical and daunting. It is the logical "next step" after the celebration of Pentecost: having moved through Lent and Easter, a movement climaxing with the outpouring of the Holy Spirit, it makes sense that we should step back and acknowledge the unity of Father, Son and Spirit that lies behind the sacred history that the Liturgical Year has just unfolded. But such a perspective is also daunting: like the incarnation, the Trinity is precisely one of those parts of our faith that escapes reason's grasp. How to pray and preach about so full a mystery in a single celebration? As always, the selections from Scripture give us points of entry that can freshen mind and imagination as we revisit this part of the heart of our faith.

John 3:16 is possibly the most familiar chapter-and-verse citation in the world. In North America at least, we meet "John 3:16" on billboards, bumper stickers, and even on placards appearing at major sports events broadcast on national television. It is easy to understand why. "For God so loved the world that he gave his only Son, so that everyone who believes in him might not perish but might have eternal life"—as a one-liner, this is a powerful summation of the Gospel. Yet, powerful as it is, the single verse requires its full context to be fully understood. John 3:16 is very much part of the fabric of the Fourth Gospel. Let us restore the verse to its setting and see how that setting helps us hear those words more clearly.

"God so loved the world that he gave his only Son . . ." This is not a word spoken on the way to the cross. The import of those simple words describing the action of God—"loved" and "gave"—surely derive from the post-Easter perspective that dominates the language of the Fourth Gospel. The Father "gave" the Son not only in the incarnation but also in the giving over to death by crucifixion. Commentators have observed that the language of a father giving an only son resonates with the Jewish memory of Abraham's readiness to give his only son in sacrifice. It also catches the divine self-emptying celebrated in the hymn that Paul quotes in the second chapter of his letter to the Philippians ("though he was in the form of God, / did not regard equality with God / something to be grasped. / Rather, he emptied himself . . .," Phil 2:6-7). As in John's prologue, this hymn addresses the whole movement of divine self-revelation in the life, death, and resurrection of Jesus.

". . . so that everyone who believes in him . . . might have eternal life." *Eternal life [zōēn iōnion]* means more than our spontaneous contemporary understanding of these words suggests. In John's vocabulary, "eternal life" is not simply unending life after death. It means literally "the *eon* life"—or the life of the "age to come" already begun. It is precisely the new "born-again" or "born-from-above" life that Jesus had just been discussing with Nicodemus earlier in this third chapter of John. To have eternal life is to enter or see the kingdom of God by being born of "water and Spirit" (3:4-5). The rest of the Gospel of John leads us to see that to believe in the Son is to accept Jesus as sent by the Father to show who God is and demonstrate what life with God is all about—laying down our lives for one another as Jesus lay down his life for us. And the gift of the Spirit of God is what enables us to live that "eternal life" here and now. Eternal life is the baptized person's participation in the life of the Trinity, both before and after our biological death.

The reading from Exodus 34—with its precious description of the Lord God as "slow to anger and rich in kindness and fidelity"—is another helpful starting point for reflection on Trinity. John the Evangelist alludes to those very words in his prologue: "While the law was given through Moses, grace and truth came through Jesus Christ" (1:17). "Grace and truth" echoes "kindness and fidelity"; both phrases reflect the same Hebrew expression describing God's covenant love in Exodus 34:6. John speaks here of one gift replacing another. First God gave the gift of the law through Moses, but the fullness of covenant love was finally given through the incarnation of the eternal Son as Jesus of Nazareth.

Finally, Paul's blessing of the Corinthians reminds us that the normal peace and harmony of Christian community is a matter of collaboration with the Trinity: "The grace of the Lord Jesus Christ and the love of God and the fellowship of the holy Spirit be with you all!"

Body and Blood of Christ

Readings: Deut 8:2-3, 14b-16a; 1 Cor 10:16-17; John 6:51-58

"Because the loaf of bread is one, we, though many,
are one body, for we all partake of the one loaf."
(1 Cor 10:17)

DISCERNING THE BODY

"Do you Christians really believe that you are eating Jesus' flesh and drinking his blood? That sounds like cannibalism." I remember my shock when I first heard that kind of question and observation coming from someone who was clearly a nonbeliever, an outsider. Having grown up with a sense of the Real Presence at the heart of my faith, the language of eating flesh and drinking blood had never even suggested cannibalism to me. But on hearing the question, I realized that, from the outsider's point of view, the question was an obvious one and deserved an answer. I came up with something like this: "We don't think of ourselves as consuming a dead body. The Eucharist is the way the risen Christ makes himself sacramentally available to us. Through this physical sign we encounter the risen Lord really present under the appearances of bread and wine."

I still think that was a pretty good answer. But now, having studied John 6, especially the part that appears as this Sunday's Gospel, I realize that there is even more to the eating and drinking language in this passage. The context of the "eucharistic discourse" of John 6 entails an important Jewish tradition that still goes largely unnoticed in current teaching and preaching.

Anyone looking for the Eucharist in the Fourth Gospel soon discovers that there is no mention of Jesus' words linking the bread and cup with his Body and Blood in John's rendition of the Last Supper. In that scene the evangelist has chosen to focus entirely on Jesus' washing of the disciples' feet. John has chosen another place to elaborate the meaning of eucharistic eating and drinking—the discourse in the Capernaum synagogue just after the feeding of the five thousand and the walking on the water. With the miracle of bread in the wilderness and Jesus' own discourse about himself being greater than manna setting the stage, the primary background here is the biblical tradition of Moses leading people to the God-given manna in the desert.

These references evoke a Jewish tradition that, while little known to today's readers, must have been well known to the original audience of this Gospel. It is the tradition that understood the manna as a symbol of God's gift of the Torah to his people.

This Sunday's selection from Deuteronomy 8 takes us to the origin of that tradition: "[God] therefore let you be afflicted with hunger, and then fed you with manna . . . in order to show you that not by bread alone does man live, but by every word that comes forth from the mouth of the LORD" (Deut 8:3). How was God's word in the Torah like manna? The human spirit hungers for the wisdom of how to live according to the will of God, for knowing what to believe and how to act in ways that find peace with God. Torah, God's self-revelation of God's self and will, is therefore truly bread in the wilderness.

Given this traditional association of manna with the Word of God in the Torah, it is powerful, then, to say that Jesus is the true bread from heaven. Now it is Jesus—the eternal Word made flesh—who is the full revelation of divine communication to the world. To know Jesus, and to receive him as sent by the Father, is to receive the fullness of God's wisdom.

Within this discourse, then, is the language of eating and drinking first about wisdom? Or is it about Eucharist? The best answer seems to be that the discourse is mainly about Jesus being God's Word made flesh, true manna from heaven; and then this Sunday's Gospel joins that understanding with the Church's practice of Eucharist. For it is in our celebration of the Eucharist that we especially encounter Jesus as God's wisdom made flesh for us. As we read further in the Fourth Gospel, we learn that to accept Jesus as sent by the Father to serve us means that we are to wash one another's feet, to lay down our lives for one another.

Paul, writing to the Corinthians, has his own way of speaking of the eucharistic body that points in the same direction. First, he asserts that the community's sharing in the Body and Blood of Christ—sharing in the one loaf—makes us one body (1 Cor 10:17). A chapter later (11:29), he says that it is absolutely crucial that we "discern the body." Here, the context makes it clear that he means "body" in two senses: (1) We need to discern that the bread and wine is the presence of the same Lord who died for us; (2) we need to discern that the community of those who share in this worship are themselves one body, requiring that we reverence one another as the body of Christ and attend to one another's needs.

Seventh Sunday of the Year

Readings: Lev 19:1-2; 17-18; 1 Cor 3:16-23; Matt 5:38-48

> **"You shall love your neighbor as yourself.**
> **I am the LORD." (Lev 19:18)**

DOES JESUS WANT DOORMATS FOR DISCIPLES?

The Gospel we read today takes us to the heart of the moral teaching of Jesus—his call to nonviolence and love of enemies. This part of the Sermon on the Mount is couched in such startling language that it has often been misunderstood. Take the sayings on nonviolence. First, consider the eye-for-an-eye rule of the Hebrew Bible (Exod 21:24, quoted in Matt 5:38). That was a good law. In the Ancient Near East, a common way to settle perceived injustices was unmitigated vengeance (you injure my brother's eye and I and my brothers will take out both of yours—maybe even kill you). So the Mosaic law of an *eye*-for-an-eye was meant to mitigate that instinct for unbridled retaliation. Moreover, Jewish legal procedure soon developed the practice of substituting financial recompense as the appropriate response to claims of personal injury—much like our practice today in the Western world.

As reasonable as that approach was, Jesus called for an even further advance against the human zest for "getting even"—which is where the famous "turn the other cheek" saying comes in. A puzzlement to most Christians, this saying has been an occasion of mockery on the part of the enemies of Christianity, as in "Why follow someone who teaches you to be a bunch of wimps and doormats?"

But that is to miss the point. We need a cultural context to catch the meaning of Jesus' example. In a mainly right-handed world, a slap across the right cheek is back-handed, and in first-century Palestine a back-handed slap was meant not so much to inflict physical injury as to dishonor the person slapped. If someone dishonored you with the demeaning back-handed slap, you were expected to reclaim your honor by responding in kind. Thus Jesus' suggestion would, in that context, be a surprising move, indicating that you simply refuse to be dishonored so easily.

The second example presents a similar ploy. The situation of someone taking someone else to court over a tunic is one of extreme oppression. After all, Exodus 22:26-27 commands: "If you take your neighbor's cloak as a pledge, you shall return it to him before sunset, for this cloak of his is the only covering he has for his body." So the oppressor is asking for something that violates the rights of the other. When Jesus suggests handing over the cloak as well, he is saying, in effect, "When you hand over your other garment, your nakedness will expose not only your flesh but also the extent of your adversary's oppression."

Similarly, the example of "going the extra mile" also draws from a specific social context. The usual way for Jesus' contemporaries to be "pressed into service" was when they were enlisted by one of the occupying Roman soldiers to carry his backpack for him. For obvious reasons, this situation was a constant source of hostility between the occupying forces and the local people. One could paraphrase Jesus' example this way: "Does that bug you when the Roman soldiers make you carry their baggage? Well, let me suggest an alternative to the hostile response you may be tempted to give: Carry it not just for the one mile but for two. That way, the Roman will get into trouble with his superior officer. He'd be exceeding his own Roman law, which allows him to press you into service for only one mile."

Thus, these sayings of Jesus are not new rules, but examples of nonviolent response to oppression. Rather than actions to be imitated literally, they were examples meant to stimulate similar forms of creative nonviolence. These teachings of Jesus inspired Mahatma Gandhi to his famous salt march, exposing the oppression of British taxation. Closer to our own time and place, these teachings of Jesus led Martin Luther King Jr. to his creative nonviolent practices of bus boycotts and restaurant sit-ins.

Taken by itself, the last line of this Sunday's Gospel can have a paralyzing effect: "So be perfect, just as your heavenly Father is perfect." The mandate is so overwhelmingly absolute, it is enough to make one crawl back into bed. How can any of us hope to be perfect as God? Few of us can even cook a good meal. But, here again, attention to context helps us get the point. Jesus is not speaking of some kind of impossible flawlessness. The previous sentences speak of the inclusiveness of the Creator's love as demonstrated in the universality of the gifts of sunshine and rain. It is precisely that quality of God's universal love that we are to imitate. Not that this is not a daunting challenge, but at least attention to the context helps us focus on the point. Those who are still hypnotized by the word "perfection" might be encouraged by Luke's version of the saying, which some scholars feel is the more original: "Be *merciful,* just as [also] your Father is merciful" (Luke 6:36).

Paul's exhortation to the Corinthian community in the second reading provides another statement that is often badly misunderstood because people usually miss the context: "Do you not know that you are the temple of God, and that the Spirit of God dwells in you? If anyone destroys God's temple, God will destroy that person; for the temple of God, which you are, is holy" (1 Cor 3:16-17). Because people commonly recall that Paul elsewhere uses the temple image for the human body (see 1 Cor 6:19, where the topic is sexual abuse), they think this statement is about individual human bodies. But the topic here in 1 Corinthians 3 is something else entirely. Here Paul is addressing the problem of factions that are destroying the body of the community (and the "you" is plural).

Attention to the contexts of today's readings help us realize that Jesus' challenge to nonviolence and love of enemies is profoundly challenging, but not impossible.

Eighth Sunday of the Year

Readings: Isa 49:14-15; 1 Cor 4:1-5; Matt 6:24-34

> **"But seek first the kingdom [of God]**
> **and his righteousness, and all these things**
> **will be given you besides." (Matt 6:33)**

To Care and Not to Care

Does Jesus invite his followers to take on the attitude of the "flower children" of the 1960s? It is not hard to hear that mentality in today's reading from the Sermon on the Mount. But what would it mean to take these words seriously?

> Why are you so anxious about clothes? Learn from the way the wild flowers grow. They do not work or spin. But I tell you that not even Solomon in all his splendor was clothed like one of them. If God so clothes the grass of the field, which grows today and is thrown into the oven tomorrow, will he not much more provide for you, O you of little faith? (Matt 6:28-30).

A single mother, struggling to raise two children on a less-than-living wage, what is she to make of such talk? The issues of providing sufficient food and clothing for herself and her children are very practical concerns for her, and she knows they are going to demand some work on her part. What possible meaning could this Sunday's Gospel have for her?

The key to understanding this radical teaching on anxiety lies in verse 33: "But seek first the kingdom [of God] and his righteousness, and all these things will be given you besides." So Jesus is not teaching us to be careless, but to center our care in the right place—on the kingdom of God. And it is important to recognize that "kingdom of God" (or "kingdom of heaven," as it more frequently appears in this Gospel) does not refer primarily to life after death but to living in response to God's reign here and now. The previous portion of the Sermon on the Mount has been all about the righteousness of God's kingdom. The righteousness mentioned in the Beatitudes (which we are to hunger and thirst for, and even suffer for) is the righteousness that must exceed that of the scribes and Pharisees (5:20). The rest of Matthew 5 spells that out as a way of life entailing forgiveness, nonviolence, and love of enemies. And the Last Judgment scenario of Matthew 25 will illustrate righteous behavior with the examples of feeding the hungry, clothing the naked, and giving drink to the thirsty.

Still, where does all this good thought leave the single mother struggling to feed and clothe her kids? It can help a little by calling her to focus her deepest care on living the life of righteousness spelled out in the whole Gospel. But perhaps the most important element in the Sermon is the aspect most frequently overlooked in the contemporary North Atlantic community—the fact that the Sermon on the Mount is addressed not simply to individuals but to the whole People of God. A community that *together* seeks first the kingdom of God and his righteousness will see to it that such mothers and their children will have the food, drink and clothing that they need.

Notice that this section of the Sermon is headed by the saying, "You cannot serve God and mammon." The poor are not often caught in the dilemma of trying to serve both God and money. It is those well off who are tempted to move beyond a balanced sufficiency to greater affluence. It is to those of us in that comfortable situation that Jesus' words are most pointedly directed. To those who find themselves caught between God and mammon Jesus says, most pertinently, "Get your priorities straight!" "Seek first the kingdom of God, and his righteousness."

For those who have the means, it is one thing to eat a healthy diet, to get enough exercise, and to dress appropriately; it is something else to be preoccupied with dietary and sartorial fashion in ways that distract one from honoring God and serving the needs of others.

Somewhere, T. S. Eliot wrote this prayerful line: "Teach us to care and not to care." This is a wise paraphrase of today's Gospel. Teach us to care enough about the kingdom so that we can cease to care so much about our own personal stuff. That way, the reign of God will become more evident, when it is embodied in a community meeting the needs of all its members.

Ninth Sunday of the Year

Readings: Deut 11:18, 26-28; Rom 3:21-25, 28; Matt 7:21-27

"Everyone who listens to these words of mine and acts on them will be like a wise man who built his house on rock." (Matt 7:24)

Impossible Dream? Or Plan of Action?

Both presentations of Jesus' great inaugural sermon—the Sermon on the Mount in Matthew 5–7 and the Sermon on the Plain in Luke 6—climax with the parable of the wise and foolish builders. One built his house on rock and it held firm under rain, flood and winds; the other built on sand and his house failed to survive rain, floods, and winds. "And great was the fall of it," says the King James Version.

Modern psychology can help us appreciate the power of Jesus' use of symbol here. People who have studied the symbols that recur in our dreams have identified the house as one of the most primal symbols of them all. There is a strong consensus that when we dream of a house we are symbolizing ourselves, and the condition of the house (chaotic? ordered? in disrepair? secure? easy to get lost in? familiar and easy to move around in?) reflects how we are doing at the present moment in the project of our lives.

What a perfect symbol, then, for Jesus to speak of a life lived wisely (a house built on rock—like the Jerusalem Temple) and a life lived foolishly (a house built on sand). And he is quite clear about what makes the difference: to build well is to hear the words of Jesus (especially as spoken in this Sermon on the Mount) and to do them; and to build foolishly is to hear the words of Jesus but fail to do them. To obey Jesus is to make an enduring success of one's life; to fail to heed Jesus is to turn one's life project into complete failure.

What gives this stark either/or image a special poignancy is the set of sayings that immediately precede this concluding parable of the builders.

Not everyone who says to me, "Lord, Lord" will enter the kingdom of heaven, but only the one who does the will of my Father in heaven. Many will say to me on that day, "Lord, Lord, did we not prophesy in your name? Did we not drive out demons in your name? Did we not do mighty deeds in your name?" Then I will declare to them solemnly, "I never knew you. Depart from me, you evildoers" (Matt 7:21-23).

Two things come through loud and clear. First, what the parable of the two builders refers to as hearing the words of Jesus is nothing less than learning the will of God. (Hence the aptness of the choice for the first reading this Sunday, Deuteronomy's celebration of the Word of God, leading to blessing for those who obey, and to a cursing for those who do not obey.) Thus, to do the will of God is to do what Jesus says, especially in the Sermon on the Mount. The second thing that this passage drives home is the startling possibility (and reality!) that one can be involved in a powerful ministry in the name of Jesus (prophecy, deliverance, and wonders!) and still be building on sand, if one fails to hear the words of Jesus and do them.

Over the centuries Christians have discussed whether the powerful challenges of the Sermon on the Mount are an impossible dream meant to humble us, or a plan of action meant to be carried out. Once we recognize that the Sermon, in both Matthew's and Luke's setting, is addressed to a community made up of people who experienced the Lord's healing, it becomes easier to see that the challenges are meant to be taken seriously. We really are meant to live forgivingly, chastely, faithfully, truthfully, nonviolently, and to love even our enemies. And failing to do so is to build on sand and make of our lives a cursed disaster.

If we find this way of speaking too starkly dramatic and threatening, we can be encouraged by the second reading, where Paul reminds the Roman Christians that any righteousness we have is a gift of God. The grace of God in Jesus can enable a community of believers to do the will of God, even as it is outlined in the Sermon on the Mount.

Tenth Sunday of the Year

Readings: Hos 6:6; Rom 4:18-25; Matt 9:9-13

**"Go and learn the meaning of the words,
'I desire mercy, not sacrifice' . . ." (Matt 9:13)**

EATING AROUND

It is hard for us to appreciate the shock value of Jesus' habit of sharing table fellowship with tax collectors and "sinners." It helps to recall that in the cultures of the Ancient Near East sharing a meal was an act of greater intimacy than we accord it in contemporary North America. Breaking bread with another was enough to seal a contract in that time and place. For the most part, our eating customs are more casual affairs.

Yet even we recognize levels of intimacy in our dining. It is one thing to take persons to lunch, another thing to take them to dinner, and still a more intimate matter to have them over to our house for supper. If even we retain some residual sensibility around table fellowship, think of what it meant for Jesus to dine so readily with the outcasts of his own day. In first-century Palestine, breaking bread with persons who were unclean by virtue of profession (such as being a tax collector for the Romans) or failure to observe the full Torah (the "sinners" Matthew refers to) was to render oneself unclean.

It is clear from Jesus' deliberate choice to violate this table taboo that this behavior was another of his prophetic symbolic actions. His meal fellowship with tax collectors and sinners was part and parcel of his kingdom preaching. And the point of it surfaces in his response to the complaint of the Pharisees in today's Gospel. It is fascinating that the one place he compares himself to a physician is not the context of physical healing but in this matter of "eating around" with tax collectors and sinners: "Those who are well do not need a physician, but the sick do." So he understands his way of including the excluded in his meal practice as a kind of healing ministry.

To this rationale the evangelist adds another not found in the other Gospels. The explanation comes in the form of a quotation from our first reading: "Go and learn the meaning of the words, 'I desire mercy, not sacrifice'" (cf. Hos 6:6). If you are like me, you can hear that verse for years and wonder why Jesus should let mercy *replace* sacrifice. "Isn't some kind of sacrifice (along with mercy, of course) essential to religious integrity?" I thought. That is because I was thinking of the self-sacrifice that the whole New Testament calls for (as in Paul's "offer your bodies as a living sacrifice" [Rom 12:1]).

Then, finally, I came to recognize that Jesus (or the evangelist) was quoting Hosea 6:6, where the poetic parallelism makes it clear that the reference is to ritual sacrifice of the Temple liturgy ("For it is love that I desire, not sacrifice, / and knowledge of God rather than holocausts"). Compassion is more important than holocausts. That is precisely what Jesus also affirmed in the Sermon on the Mount, when he taught that anyone about to make an offering at the Temple and remembering that he is not reconciled with his brother should leave the offering at the altar and first go and be reconciled, and only then come and offer the gift (Matt 5:23-24).

Whether this application of Hosea 6:6 to Jesus' table fellowship comes from Matthew, or from the pre-Gospel tradition, or from Jesus himself, there is no doubt it reflects Jesus' teaching and illuminates his behavior. If one's worship of God is not reflected in the quality of one's relationships with other human beings, the worship is empty. This is an important passage to reflect on at a time when candidates for political office can speak with unction about "Christian values" and at the same time promote policies that prevent millions of citizens from taking a decent seat at the table of this nation's abundance.

Eleventh Sunday of the Year

Readings: Exod 19:2-6; Rom 5:6-11; Matt 9:36-10:8

> **"Therefore, if you hearken to my voice and keep my
> covenant, you shall be my special possession,
> dearer to me than all other people,
> though all the earth is mine.
> You shall be to me a kingdom of priests,
> a holy nation."(Exod 19:5-6)**

PRIESTLY PEOPLE

Was it Jesus' original aim to found a new religion? Anyone who thinks so will find that understanding challenged by this Sunday's Gospel. For in Jesus' commissioning of the Twelve, all of the language is about the restoration of Israel, not the creation of a new people. Renewal, not innovation, is the theme here.

First, Jesus has deliberately chosen an inner core of *twelve*. Recall that Israel had ceased being a twelve-tribe unity ever since the split into the northern and southern kingdoms in the late tenth century. They were further scattered by the Assyrian conquest in the eighth century and the Babylonian Exile in the sixth century. The restoration of the scattered twelve tribes was part of Jewish hope for the messianic "age to come." Thus, Jesus' choice of twelve leaders symbolized that they were engaged in the end-time restoration of the people of Israel.

The description of the people as "troubled and abandoned, like sheep without a shepherd," resonates with key moments in Israel's past. Numbers 27:17 uses that description of the people of Israel to highlight the need for leadership when God tells Moses to commission Joshua to lead them into the Promised Land. Later, Ezekiel will speak of the exiles as sheep "scattered for lack of a shepherd" (Ezek 34:5). Jesus' evocation of that image as he commissions the Twelve suggests that Israel is still a people in exile and on the verge of entering a new Promised Land.

Jesus' description of the mission as a "harvest" and God as "the harvest master" strikes another end-time chord. For later on in this Gospel, Jesus will speak of the "end of the age" as a harvest (13:39).

Finally, Jesus empowers the Twelve to heal and to preach that the kingdom of God is at hand. In short, Jesus commissions the twelve apostles to do precisely what he had been doing— announcing to "the lost sheep of the house of Israel" the arrival of the long-awaited intervention of the reign of God and demonstrating that arrival through the ministry of healing.

The Gospel of Matthew goes on to record that the project of renewing the house of Israel was only partially successful. The upshot, however, is not withdrawal but expansion. The finale of Matthew's Gospel consists in the Great Commission of the risen Lord to those lost sheep who allow themselves to be found, represented by the diminished and hesitant "eleven," to go and make disciples of all nations.

This mission of Israel to bring the Good News of God's coming in power to all nations finds support in what may seem an unexpected place, today's first reading, Exodus 19—God's words to Moses at Sinai regarding Israel's call: "You shall be to me a kingdom of priests, a holy nation." There is mission in those words. For they imply a powerful analogy: as the Temple priesthood is to Israel, so shall Israel be to "all the earth." In other words, as a priest is a mediator between the God and Israel, so you as a people are to be mediators between God and all the nations—a "light to the nations," in Isaiah's terms.

The commission of the Twelve to join Jesus' effort to renew Israel brings home two important realities. First, we (for the most part, Gentile) disciples of Jesus are beneficiaries of God's covenant with the house of Israel, and therefore will always have a special relationship with Jews around the world. Second, our own task of evangelization will include the renewal of our own people of faith as much as an outreach to the unchurched.

Twelfth Sunday of the Year

Readings: Jer 20:10-13; Rom 5:12-15; Matt 10:26-33.

> **"And do not be afraid of those who kill the body but cannot kill the soul; rather, be afraid of the one who can destroy both soul and body in Gehenna."**
> **(Matt 10:28)**

THE FEAR THAT FREES

Fear God? This Sunday's Gospel flies in the face of what many current preachers and teachers take for granted is their task: to help people get over their fear of God.

Jesus says just the opposite. On the one hand, after predicting a time in which his disciples will experience their state as being like "sheep in the midst of wolves" (10:16), undergoing scourgings, being handed over to death by family members, Jesus says not to be afraid of such people. They can only kill the body but cannot touch the soul. On the other hand, Jesus says, "Be afraid of the one who can destroy both soul and body in Gehenna." In other words, fear God. But rather than leave us with that bald statement, Jesus hastens to add a thought "on the third hand": God whose eye is on the sparrow, cares even more for you. Indeed, he even counts the hairs on your head. So do not be afraid. You are worth much more than a whole flock of sparrows.

Did the third hand take away what the second hand gave? Jesus is saying that the One who holds the ultimate power over you is the One who loves you the most. How, then, does exhortation to fear God apply? Jesus is here simply recalling a theme deep in the Hebrew tradition, the intimate connection between fear and love of God (see Deut 10:12; Pss 33:18; 103:11, 17; 118:4; Prov 16:6). What is meant by fear in these contexts is a complete awe and reverence for the Creator, such that one always acts out of profound respect for this Maker, Rescuer, Sustainer, and Judge of all.

If "fear" of God has such a positive meaning, why, then, does Scripture insist on negative words that are best translated "fear" in this case? Analogy may help. Every parent wants to instill in a toddler a healthy fear of fire, deep water, and automobile traffic. Not to respect the danger of such things is to be dangerously out of touch. This is not the craven fear that would keep the child from eventually learning to cook, to swim, and to drive a car. It is a healthy fear that instills a respect for the power of such things. Similarly, biblical fear of God is a deep sense of God's otherness and ultimacy, such that all of our actions are governed by our wonder and respect for this powerful Other.

Perhaps a more helpful analogy is the fear we have of offending those we love the most. Are we not deeply pained when we discover that a word or act of ours has hurt a parent, a child, or a good friend? And do we not fear offending them? That's the fear Jesus would have us feel toward the Father. When our love life is governed by this fear of God, we discover that we really have nothing to be afraid of. "Perfect love drives out fear" (1 John 4:18).

Thirteenth Sunday of the Year

Readings: 2 Kgs 4:8-11, 14-16; Rom 6:3-4, 8-11: Matt 10:37-42

"Whoever finds his life will lose it, and whoever loses his life for my sake will find it." (Matt 10:39)

GETTING A LIFE

When a pharmaceutical company says, "Live well!" we know their blessing envisions a judicious use of their products to enhance our remaining years on this earth. When the beer people remind us that we "only go round once," we know that they want us to include an enjoyment of their product as we try to squeeze the most pleasure out of this short life. And when the cotton people show us touching video clips of joyful family moments while a soulful voice sings about "the fabric of our lives," we know whose fabric they want us to be wearing during these special times. In each case, the language of life points to the biological life that ends, sooner than we expect, in death.

How remarkably different is the language of life that we find in Scripture! While the Bible acknowledges the goodness and shortness of biological life, it also makes bold to stretch the words we use for life and death and apply them in a fresh way to the death-defying covenant life we share with God. And it does so in a way that must sound to the uninitiated like double talk—as, for example, in the saying of Jesus quoted at the head of this column (whoever finds his life will lose it). This is worth a closer look.

When we hear Jesus, in his mission charge to the Twelve, say, "Whoever finds his life will lose it, and whoever loses his life for my sake will find it," we know that we are hearing paradox. And paradox forces us to make sense of the language by taking it beyond the obvious sense. If we wonder in what sense "finding life" constitutes loss, we get help from Matthew 16:25-26: "For whoever wishes to save his life will lose it, but whoever loses his life for my sake will find it. What profit would there be for one to gain the whole world and forfeit his life?" In that context, the false "finding" of life is the result of misguided life-saving efforts such as gaining more and more possessions, whereas the life that one gains by losing it for the sake of Jesus is the everlasting life of the kingdom of God—which does indeed begin in this biological life but perdures beyond biological death.

When Paul writes to the Romans about his understanding of the change that occurs in baptism, he indulges in the same paradoxical language that Jesus used. It helps to recall that Paul is reflecting on a ritual that involved, in his day, the total immersion in water of the baptized person. That complete immersion symbolized, first of all, not cleansing but dying. The baptized person dies to sinful solidarity with Adam and then, surfacing to breathe air once again, rises to share in the new life of the risen Christ, the life of the Christian community. Paul shares with the Fourth Gospel a way of understanding Christian life as a new level of existence, such that he, like John, can say that the Christian has already passed through death and now shares in an eternal life that biological death is unable to interrupt.

This Sunday's readings invite us to reflect on another dimension of that life, hospitality. When the Shunammite woman extends to the prophet Elisha the generous hospitality of having a special guest room especially for him, she is rewarded with an unexpected gift of life: her sterility is healed and she conceives and bears a son. And even when that son dies an early death, she receives the surprising gift of his resuscitation. Jesus' mission discourse concludes with words elaborating that theme of hospitality and its rewards. Jesus assures his disciples that mission in his name will involve them in an adventure of hospitality that will bless abundantly those that receive them. As in the case of the Shunammite woman and Elisha, Jesus promises, "whoever receives a prophet because he is a prophet, receives a prophet's reward." An even larger context is revealed in the words "whoever receives you receives me, and whoever receives me receives the one who sent me" (10:40). In other words, Christian mission and hospitality is nothing less than living out a relationship with God. Life becomes larger than it seems.

The Gospel vision denies none of the goodness of beer, cotton, and good medicine in this short biological life, but it asserts a broad network of relationships that exceeds the limitations of biological life and requires us to stretch the normal meanings of our human language about life and death. The invitation of Jesus rinses the sarcasm out of the contemporary taunt, "Get a life."

Fourteenth Sunday of the Year

Readings: Zech 9:9-10; Rom 8:9, 11-13; Matt 11:25-30

**"The warrior's bow shall be banished,
and he shall proclaim peace to the nations." (Zech 9:10)**

BANISHING THE BOW

If there is any part of the Gospel that sounds like a call to withdraw from involvement with the world around us, it is today's selection from Matthew. With its talk of coming as children to the meek and gentle one who will ease our burdens and refresh our spirits, it appeals to our desire to draw back from the fray and allow ourselves to be healed. Indeed, there are times in life when we need to hear those words in just that way. But when we step back and read the rest of the Gospel of Matthew, looking for ways that spell out the implications of following the meek and gentle master, we hear a disturbing challenge. The first chapter of the Sermon on the Mount calls healed disciples to live a life of forgiveness, of disciplining the impulses of anger and lust, of absolute honesty, of love of enemies, and of responding to violence with creative nonviolence. This helps us see what Jesus means by his burden and his yoke.

The reading from Zechariah recalls and helps us understand a symbolic action Jesus used when he wanted to correct people's misunderstanding of his messiahship. It seems that the main image of Messiah in the minds of Jesus' contemporaries was modeled after King David. The Anointed One of the Age to Come would be a warrior like David of old. Such a "son of David" would enable them to overthrow the Roman power that was oppressing them. According to the Synoptic writers, Jesus prepared carefully a symbolic action meant to counter such expectations regarding his role. He arranged to have a donkey ready on which to enter Jerusalem. As Matthew takes pains to explain, this gesture was meant to recall Zechariah 9:9, the prophecy about a nonviolent king who would banish the instruments of war from Jerusalem.

Nonviolence is an aspect of Jesus' teaching and action that we have too easily neglected over the centuries. At this time of year, when we commemorate our Declaration of Independence and the military activity that implemented that independence, it is a good time to acknowledge that the Lord calls us now to use our freedom to serve the world in ways that honor a consistent ethic of life, and to strive to find alternatives to abortion, the death penalty, and the use of military force to resolve political problems.

Fifteenth Sunday of the Year

Readings: Isa 55:10-11; Rom 8:18-23; Matt 13:1-23

"Whoever has ears ought to hear." (Matt 13:9)

CRACKING A PARABLE

If you were a first-century Palestinian peasant and you heard this craftsman-turned-prophet from Nazareth speak about the sower who went out to sow and got those mixed results (some seed lost to birds, some to sunburn, some to encroaching weeds, and finally some seed finding good ground and sprouting), how would you know you are supposed to hear this as a parable—a story that presents an image of something else? Maybe the man in the boat is just talking about how tough it is to farm in the stony, weedy, bird-bedeviled Palestinian soil. Would your response be, maybe, "Yup, that's agriculture"? If you were alert and soil-smart, you might pick up on at least two cues hinting that the story points beyond itself. First, the seed falling on the good soil produces a surprisingly abundant harvest: whereas the usual yield is ten seeds up for every one seed down, these seeds give 100, 60, and 30 seeds for every single seed put down. As an experienced farmer, you would notice this amazing contrast between the unpromising beginnings (seed squelched by birds, sun, and weeds) and the fantastic harvest that eventually emerges.

Second, you would likely have picked up on Jesus' saying, "Whoever has ears to hear ought to hear." What's to hear? It must be a meaning beyond the obvious. Taking your lead from the talk of seed that achieves, willy-nilly, a successful harvest, and searching for the symbolic possibilities of that imagery, you just might recall the passage from Isaiah 55, this Sunday's first reading. There the prophet compares the effectiveness of God's word with the natural processes of rain and snow nurturing the growth and fruitfulness of seeds.

Applying this imagery to the present situation of the prophet addressing you from the boat, you might hear him telling you something like this: "Folks, this might not seem like much, a rag-tag group of out-casts drawn to me by my stories and healing, but just you wait. This God-movement is eventually going to grow enormously." Jesus, then, would be the sower, and the seed nothing less than the word of God.

The disciples may or may not have caught all this. As Matthew tells it, when they ask Jesus about the parable, he supplies another text from Isaiah (Isa 6:9-10) to explain what was hindering a fuller reception of his word—gross hearts, and ears and eyes that are spiritually deaf and blind.

Then Jesus proceeds to spell out an allegorical interpretation that names what blocks full growth of the word—failing to understand what was sown in the heart, being shallow in one's response and there-fore wilting in the face of persecution, and being distracted by worldly anxiety and desire for riches.

That is all clear enough, but what sometimes confuses careful read-ers is the apparent confusion about what the seed represents. Verse 19 seems to say that the seed is both "the word of the kingdom" and the *person* who responds (poorly or well). As the explanation continues, the emphasis is on the seed as person: e.g., "The seed sown on the rocky ground is the one who hears the word and receives it at once with joy" (v. 20). We might like a clear equation, either seed = the word, *or* seed = person. But the biblical tradition gives precedent for seed symbolizing both of those meanings. Isaiah 55 associates seed with the word of God, but Hosea 2:23 and Jeremiah 31:27 use the sowing image for a renewed people. So there is reason to make seed serve as a double-duty symbol. Indeed, Matthew, in the scene immediately preceding this parable's discourse, has provided an episode illustrating how a community of people is created by their response to the word of God. When Jesus is told that his mother and brothers are standing outside asking to speak with him, Jesus stretches out his hand toward his disciples, and says, "Here are my mother and my brothers. For whoever does the will of my heavenly Father is my brother, and sister, and mother" (12:49-50).

Sixteenth Sunday of the Year

Readings: Wis 12:13, 16-19; Rom 8:26-27; Matt 13:24-43

> **"Let them grow together until harvest;**
> **then at harvest time I will say to the harvesters,**
> **'First collect the weeds and tie them in bundles for burning;**
> **but gather the wheat into my barn.'" (Matt 13:30)**

THE WHEAT AND THE WEEDS

In the story of the wheat and the weeds we have another parable for which Matthew supplies an allegorical interpretation. As in the case of the parable of the Sower, familiarity with the allegorical application can prevent us from hearing the story in another good way, namely as a story on its own, probably the way Jesus first told it.

As we did with the Sower, before we move to the application, let's try to hear the "Wheat and the Tares" as it might have been heard during Jesus' ministry. First, it is helpful to know that the weed named here is a particular kind *(zizania)* known for its confusing resemblance to wheat in the early stages of growth. That helps us to understand why pulling up the weeds might uproot the wheat along with them. What, then, is the point of the farmer saying, "Let them grow together until harvest; then at harvest time I will say to the harvester, 'First collect the weeds and tie them in bundles for burning; but gather the wheat into my barn'"?

On one immediate level, this could simply be a story of a clever man getting the better of his enemy. The enemy thought he was duping the land owner into ripping up his crop along with the weeds, but our cool farmer says, in effect, "No, let them both grow together; then we'll have a double harvest—a fuel crop (the weeds, which can be burned) and a food crop (the grain)." The tale could well have had a prior existence as this kind of story, something like a fable from Aesop. But the context here in Matthew's Gospel calls for something more that fits the setting of Jesus' ministry or that of the Church. Such a meaning might be this: Don't you try to judge the righteous and unrighteous of the community; let them grow together till the end, when God will take care of the final sorting out.

Notice that the interpretation that Matthew supplies moves the center of gravity to the judgment scene, where the Son of Man sends angels to collect for punishment evildoers, even out of his kingdom. Thus, what may at first have been a plea to church leaders for restraint in judgment becomes a cautionary tale for us all.

Seventeenth Sunday of the Year

Readings: 1 Kgs 3:5, 7-12; Rom 8:28-30; Matt 13:44-52

"The kingdom of heaven is like a treasure buried in a field, which a person finds and hides again, and out of joy goes and sells all that he has and buys that field." (Matt 13:44)

First Comes the Finding

"Wait a minute," you may want to say. "If the person finds the treasure on someone else's property, doesn't it belong to the owner? Consequently, isn't the finder acting deceptively?" This is a needless distraction. Since the owner sells the land without adverting to buried valuables, he is obviously unaware of the stashed goods. In that time and place—before banks, safes and strongboxes—safeguarding precious items by burying them in the ground was a common practice. The scenario of this little parable implies that the finder has stumbled upon a long-forgotten treasure of which the present land owner is oblivious. But since it is indeed on someone else's property, the finder does need to purchase the land in order to claim the goods. But there is nothing un-ethical here.

A second distraction is the wording "the kingdom of heaven is like . . ." Does that mean the parable is somehow about heaven as a place, or "getting to heaven"? No, the parable is not about the kingdom which is the place called heaven, for "kingdom of heaven" is simply Matthew's preferred expression for what Mark and Luke call "the kingdom (or reign) of God." And this is first of all a reference to a rela-tionship, not a place. Recall that the reign of God in Jesus' teaching and preaching refers to the end-time coming of God to rescue his people. It is, in other words, the fresh initiative of God inaugurated through the life, death and resurrection of Jesus—and still to be fulfilled completely in the future.

Distractions cleared, the main question remains: how does the situ-ation of the person finding a treasure, and then selling all in order to possess that treasure—how does that situation show how one relates to the reign of God? The author John Dominic Crossan once wrote a little book about this parable, along with other treasure trove stories. He called it *Finding is the First Act*. And that is precisely the point. First of all, one encounters the kingdom of God as a *given*. As the first letter of John puts it, "In this is love: not that we have loved God, but that he loved us . . ." (1 John 4:10). Then, in the sheer joy of that discovery, one lets go of everything else to embrace that gift. The point of insisting that finding is the first act is that it reminds us of a truth so much stressed in Paul's letters, that God's gift is prior to human response.

Jesus says the same thing in other terms when he says, "Whoever does not accept the kingdom of God like a child will not enter it" (Mark 10:15; Luke 18:17). Receiving comes before entering, just as finding comes before the selling and buying in our parable. This parallels the experience of those who, like C. S. Lewis, describe their Christian conversion as being "surprised by joy." That dramatic experience of God's grace is a special blessing. For others, the discovering of the invitation of God's reign in their lives comes after a long search. Matthew honors their experience by coupling the story of the buried treasure with the one about the merchant who finds the pearl of great price after a long quest; but, like the one who stumbles into the buried treasure, he too "sells all that he has and buys it."

The story about King Solomon in the first reading illustrates the spirit of these parables in Solomon's prayer. Told by the Lord God to ask for anything he wants, he asks for "an understanding heart to judge your people and to distinguish right from wrong." God's answer shows that this choice indicates a willingness to "sell all," let go of everything else (long life, riches, the life of his enemies).

Simply put, these little parables are ways of reflecting on the love life of a disciple. Jesus puts it yet another way in the Sermon on the Mount when he says, "But seek first the kingdom [of God] and his righteousness, and all these things [food, clothing] will be given you besides" (6:33). Or again, "Where your treasure is, there also will your heart be" (6:21). In still other words, Paul, in this Sunday's second reading, catches both elements, divine initiative and the simplification of life that comes from "selling all" to receive the treasure: "We know that all things work for good for those who love God, who are called according to his purpose" (Rom 8:28).

To consider what "selling all" to buy the farm might mean today, ask yourself this: If the reign of God entails a consistent ethic of life—honoring the lives of the unborn, the enemy, the aging, the handicapped, the poor, the convicted—as my Church teaches, what residue of selfishness or vengeance do I need to let go of to fully embrace such an ethic?

Eighteenth Sunday of the Year

Readings: Isa 55:1-3; Rom 8:35, 37-39; Matt 14:13-21

> "'There is no need for them to go away; give them
> some food yourselves.' But they said to him,
> 'Five loaves and two fish are all we have here.'
> Then he said, 'Bring them here to me.'" (Matt 14:16-18)

Dinner and a Show?

I once heard a scholar, interviewed on a TV special about Jesus, refer to the feeding of the five thousand with the phrase "dinner and a show." His point was, I think, to characterize Jesus' ministry as "meeting folks where they are." And that is surely part of the meaning of this episode. Responding in heartfelt compassion to the people's needs, Jesus healed them and fed them. But there are other dimensions to the account as well. Characterizing the Galilean seaside as a "desert" place surely evokes the memory of Israel in the wilderness and Jesus as a new Moses mediating manna for the wanderers invited into a new Exodus. The similarity to the account in 2 Kings 4:24-44 about Elisha feeding one hundred with twenty loaves reminds us that a prophet greater than Elisha is here. And no one misses the parallel between Jesus' gestures here—taking, blessing, and breaking the loaves and giving them to his disciples—and his actions at the Last Supper. What catches my attention this time is the role of the disciples. Told to feed the people, they think only of their own meager resources. When they heed Jesus' command, "Bring them to me," the people are abundantly fed. That reminds us disciples, ordained and nonordained alike, that our part in the mission does not depend on our own poor resources but on bringing others to the feeder and healer himself, Jesus.

Nineteenth Sunday of the Year

Readings: 1 Kgs 19:9a, 11-13a; Rom 9:1-5; Matt 14:22-33

> **"Immediately Jesus stretched out his hand
> and caught Peter, and said to him,
> 'O you of little faith, why did you doubt?'" (Matt 14:31)**

WALKING ON WATER

Each of the Gospel authors has his own distinctive and consistent way of telling the story of Jesus. The episode about the walking on the water is one of the best passages for demonstrating how purposeful and meaningful those variations can be. Take a moment and read carefully first Mark's account (Mark 6:45-52) and then Matthew's (Matt 14:22-33). Did you notice that Matthew's version is about 50 percent longer (the three and a half verses devoted to Peter's failed effort to walk on water)?

And did you notice the completely opposite reactions of the disciples? In Mark's version, when Jesus gets into the boat and the wind dies down, they are astounded, and Mark observes, "They had not understood the incident of the loaves. On the contrary, their hearts were hardened" (6:52). In Matthew's version, on the other hand, after Jesus rescues Peter and both get into the boat and the wind dies down, "those who were in the boat did him homage, saying, 'Truly, you are the Son of God'" (14:32). In Mark's version, the disciples are not enlightened by this experience. In Matthew's version, however, they *worship* (that is the meaning of *prosekynēsan*) Jesus and collectively confess him to be "the Son of God"—something the disciples never come to recognize in the whole Gospel of Mark.

Each of these different reactions is consistent with the presentation of the disciples in its respective Gospel. In Mark, the twelve consistently fail to understand Jesus' teaching. Indeed, in connection with another reference to bread, their behavior prompts Jesus to ask, "Do you not yet understand or comprehend? Are your hearts hardened? Do you have eyes and not see, ears and not hear?" (Mark 8:17-18). But in Matthew's version of the conversation, Jesus does not make that critique; indeed, in Matthew they do understand about the bread (see Matt 16:12). Mark, throughout his Gospel, pictures the disciples as spiritually blind. Pointedly, Mark frames the instruction of the disciples in chapters 8 through 10 with the two cures from blindness; what the blind man of Bethsaida and blind Bartimaeus receive physically, the disciples need on the spiritual level: they fail to see that Jesus' messsiahship entails suffering.

On the other hand, Matthew consistently presents the disciples as understanding quite well; their problem is that they have little faith. In the walking-on-the-water episode, the portrait of Peter illustrates exactly that point. In the incident of the storm at sea, Jesus had berated them as being "of little faith" (Matt 8:25). If there is any uncertainty as to whether this doubting of the disciples is a special theme of Matthew's, it becomes quite clear in the final scene of his Gospel, the appearance of the risen Lord to the eleven on a mountain in Galilee. Matthew describes that encounter in a startling sentence: "When they saw him, they worshiped [*prosekynēsan*], but they doubted [*edistasan*]" (Matt 28:17). Notice that the word translated "worshiped" here is the same as the word translated "did him homage" describing the disciples' response in the water-walk scene. Equally significant, the word for "doubted" is precisely the word for Peter's doubt used in Jesus' question after he rescues the sinking man. To say that at the appearance of the risen Lord, "they worshiped, but they doubted" sounds so contradictory that most translations (e.g., KJV, Rheims, NIV, and NRSV) say "they worshiped but *some* doubted." But the NAB (1986) accurately reflects the Matthean text, a mix of faith and doubt already represented in the rescue episode of this Sunday's Gospel.

Apparently Matthew boldly addresses the shaky faith life of his readership. Like his portrait of the disciples, they have a fine understanding of Jesus and his teaching. They just need to trust in the risen Lord sufficiently to put that understanding fully into action. Would Matthew address us any differently?

Assumption (August 15)

Readings: Rev 11:19a; 12:1-6a, 10ab; 1 Cor 15:20-27; Luke 1:39-56

**"She gave birth to a son, a male child,
destined to rule all the nations with an iron rod.
Her child was caught up to God and his throne." (Rev 12:5)**

A WOMAN CLOTHED WITH THE SUN

The vision of the "woman clothed with the sun, with the moon beneath her feet, and on her head a crown of twelve stars" (Rev 12:1) is not first about Mary the mother of Jesus. In the context of Revelation, this figure, the best of Catholic biblical scholarship assures us, represents the People of God (old and new). The complex of sun, moon, and twelve stars figure in the dream of Joseph (Gen 37:9-10, where sun and moon stand for his parents and eleven stars stand for his eleven brothers, all bowing down to him, the twelfth). Woman Israel gives birth to the Messiah, after whose exaltation she continues to live (like Israel of the Exodus), endangered but divinely protected.

If the woman stands for the whole People of God, does that mean the Church's use of this text to honor Mary is biblically unwarranted? Not at all. First, the place of Mary in salvation history is surely implied in the reference to the birth of Israel's Messiah. Moreover, Mary the mother of Jesus is elsewhere treated in the Gospels as embodying the People of Israel. Indeed, the Gospel reading for this Sunday, the Magnificat, refers to the fuller history of Israel by echoing the hymn of Samuel's mother Hannah (1 Sam 2:1-10), as well as seeing her (Mary's) motherhood as God's helping "Israel his servant" and acting "according to his promise . . . to Abraham and to his descendants forever" (Luke 1:54-55). Thus, the liturgy's use of Revelation 12 to celebrate Mary is a most appropriate application of the text. Indeed, this appropriation brings about what is implicit in the text, Mary's place in God's history with Israel.

Today's first reading from Revelation further draws from Revelation by including a verse from the hymn in Revelation 12: "Now have salvation and power come, / the kingdom of our God / and the authority of his Anointed." Along with the selection from 1 Corinthians 15, this hymn places the Assumption in the fullest context. What was begun in Mary will come to fruition in nothing less than the fullness of the kingdom of God.

Twentieth Sunday of the Year

Readings: Isa 56:1, 6-7; Rom 11:13-15, 29-32; Matt 15:221-28

**"For my house shall be called
a house of prayer for all peoples." (Isa 56:7)**

THAT WOMAN IS OURSELVES

Mark calls her "a Greek" but Matthew uses the ancient name "Canaanite," a reference to the original inhabitants of the Holy Land, who were conquered by the Israelites some twelve centuries before the time of Jesus. Matthew recognizes that this encounter between the woman from the area of Tyre and Sidon and Jesus is about an outsider "wanting in." So he heightens the drama by identifying her as a member of that group of pagans who were Israel's first enemies (after the Egyptians, of course). Notwithstanding her status as "Canaanite," her anxiety about her demonized daughter brings her to Jesus with a plea that he heal her.

Matthew turns her into a model of Christian prayer when he amends Mark's version to have her say, "Have mercy on me, Lord, Son of David." Again revising Mark, Matthew introduces a startling response by Jesus: "I was sent only to the lost sheep of the house of Israel" (for this indeed was his way of operating during his earthly ministry, the Great Commission to make disciples of all the nations coming only later [Matt 28:19]). When she insists, again modeling Jewish-Christian prayer, "Lord help me," Jesus goes so far as to use a popular insult term for Gentiles: "It is not right to take the food of the children and throw it to the dogs." In turn, the woman has the blessed hutzpah to make a witty play on Jesus' image: "Please, Lord, for even the dogs eat the scraps that fall from the table of their masters." Notice that she just addressed Jesus as "master" *(Kyrie).* "O woman," he responds, "Great is your faith. Let it be done for you as you wish." And her daughter was healed from that hour.

We rightly marvel at the faith of the woman, and we wonder at the abrupt words of Jesus. But when we ask the question of why Matthew, and Mark before him, saw fit to include this account in their Gospels, it becomes evident that they, especially Matthew, had other concerns than ours. For Matthew's introduction of the reference about Jesus' mission to the house of Israel echoes the theme of Israel-first-then-the-nations developed elsewhere in his Gospel (see 10:5-6 and 28:19).

Today's first reading, from Isaiah 56, helps us appreciate that larger picture which Matthew made his own. Isaiah envisions foreigners coming to the Jerusalem Temple to "join themselves to the Lord" and to "make joyful" in God's house. This joining of foreigners in the worship of Israel is not something that occurred upon Israel's return from the Exile. Indeed there were laws against pagans even stepping into the inner court of the Temple. This oracle referred to something beyond what the returning Judahites were ready for. That is why the prophecy could so readily be understood as a reference to messianic end-times. Indeed, the vision climaxes with words that Jesus quotes on the occasion of his cleansing of the Temple toward the end of his mission: "For my house shall be called / a house of prayer for all peoples." Jesus' announcement of the kingdom of God signaled the end of business as usual, and an opening of the heritage of Israel to the rest of the world.

That's where we come in—that vast majority of us Christians who are Gentiles. However we understand the mainstream Jewish rejection of Jesus as Messiah—and the reading from Romans 11 shows that this question preoccupied Paul greatly—the fact is that Christian faith has its roots in Judaism and understands Jesus as implementing the vocation of Israel to be a light to the world. It would be a salutary help toward humility if we let the account of the Canaanite woman remind us that if we have found healing in the house of Jesus, it is only because we are foreigners who have been allowed to come in from the outside.

Twenty-First Sunday of the Year

Readings: Isa 22:19-23; Rom 11:33-36; Matt 16:13-20

> **"And so I say to you, you are Peter *[Petros]*,
> and upon this rock *[petra]* I will build my church,
> and the gates of the netherworld
> shall not prevail against it." (Matt 16:18)**

ROCK, CHIEF RABBI, MAJORDOMO

Someone, I think it was George Bernard Shaw, said, "The church was founded with a pun." He was right. The intent of that remark may have been dismissive, but, as is usual with biblical puns, the wordplay of Jesus is far from trivial. In fact, the play on Simon's nickname is just one of several rich biblical allusions at work in this key passage.

Peter was not a personal name in first-century Palestine. *Petros*, the masculine form of the Greek word *petra* ("rock"—reflected in our English words "petrify" and "petroleum," oil from rock rather than olives), translates the Aramaic *kepha* ("rock"). Kepha, or Peter, is a special name that Jesus gives Simon bar Jonah to signify his appointed mission.

Why Rock? We might call someone Rocky today to refer to his physical toughness. In Simon's case the name more likely has biblical roots. First, there is the precedent of Isaiah 51:1-2, where the founding ancestors of the people of Israel, Abraham and Sarah, are called, respectively, "the rock from which you were hewn" and "the pit from which you were quarried." Then there is the fact that the expected messiah was to be the builder of a new temple, just as in 2 Samuel 7 the son of David was to build a temple; and even though the first son of David, Solomon, built the first temple, the end-time Messiah was also expected to build the temple of the messianic age. When Jesus speaks of "building" his Church on the rock of Simon, he is of course speaking of a community, but the image is that of a physical structure, a temple. And temple does indeed become a favorite image of the early Church to describe itself (as in 1 Cor 3:10-16, 1 Pet 2:2-8, and Eph 2:19-22).

But if the Church can be pictured as temple, it is also a household. That image comes into play when Jesus speaks of giving Peter the keys to the kingdom. Isaiah 22, the first reading this Sunday, provides the background. King Hezekiah's steward has abused his office and the prophet mediates the divine command that the king is to dismiss him and bestow the key of the house of David upon Eliakim. With the language of "keys to the kingdom," Jesus appoints Peter as steward of the Church, now imaged as household—indeed, the spiritual household of the ultimate Son of David.

A further image comes into play when Jesus speaks of "binding and loosing" to describe Peter's authority. Binding and loosing refers to the authority of the chief rabbi of a community. Sometimes it referred to the application of the Torah to a particular case (the apparent reference here). Sometimes it referred to the power to include or exclude a member of the community (see Matt 18:18). Thus, Jesus makes Peter, in effect, chief rabbi of the community of the Church.

This passage has been a battleground of hostile debate between Protestants and Catholics. In some quarters it may still be that, but in today's sober dialogue between Catholic and Lutheran scholars at least, a strong consensus has emerged that the Petrine ministry of overseeing the unity of the Church (historically realized by the Bishops of Rome) is an essential part of the New Testament's presentation of the Church of Christ. And so it is part of any Christian's discipleship to pray and work for the full realization of that ministry of unity, the reunion of a divided Church.

Twenty-Second Sunday of the Year

Readings: Jer 20:7-9; Rom 12:1-2; Matt 16:21-27

> **"I urge you, brothers and sisters,
> by the mercies of God, to offer your bodies as a
> living sacrifice, holy and pleasing to God,
> your spiritual worship." (Rom 12:1)**

STUMBLING STONE, BURNING HEART, LIVING SACRIFICE

This Sunday's Gospel continues the dialogue between Jesus and Simon, the Rock on which Jesus will build his Church. What happens is, quite literally, scandalous. Jesus follows his granting of primacy to the freshly named Peter with the first prediction of his passion (and resurrection). In response Peter rebukes Jesus and says, "God forbid, Lord! No such thing shall ever happen to you." Whereupon Jesus turns to Peter with strong words: "Get behind me, Satan! You are an obstacle to me. You are thinking not as God does, but as human beings do." The word behind "obstacle" is *skandalon,* literally "stumbling block." The foundation stone has become a stumbling stone. "Satan" (adversary) is already such a shocking term that we scarcely notice *skandalon.*

Matthew (and Mark, though not Luke or John) dares to present Peter opposing Jesus in this matter of a suffering Messiah apparently because he knows that Peter eventually learns and accepts the whole truth, and even loses his own life (in Rome) witnessing to Jesus as crucified and risen. The foundation-stone-become-stumbling-stone stands as a cautionary tale for all of us who are called to serve with authority in the Church, a reality that surely extends to parents with respect to their children and teachers with respect to students. The good news is that, by the grace of God, rehabilitation is not only possible but likely, if we pray.

We know, from the Acts of the Apostles and from tradition, that Simon was indeed enabled by the grace of God to become the rock the Church needed. Like Jeremiah in today's first reading, and like another initially recalcitrant instrument (Paul), Peter was soon impelled to generous service by a fire in the belly.

Paul himself, in the reading from Romans, supplies a stunning image for Christian service that deserves our attention. "Offer your bodies," he writes, "as a living sacrifice, holy and pleasing to God, your spiritual worship." As Jesus drew from Temple tradition to speak of building on a rock, Paul too draws from the realm of the Temple. Israel's practice had been to offer up the bodies of dead animals in Temple worship. Now Paul—in the spirit of Isaiah, Micah, and Psalm 51—says that the best offering to God is not a dead animal body but your own living one, not in suicidal immolation but in the very living out of your life. The rest of Romans 12 spells that out as building up the body of the Church by using one's gifts in mutual service, hospitality, prayer, and love of enemies.

Twenty-Third Sunday of the Year

Readings: Ezek 33:7-9; Rom 13:8-10; Matt 18:15-20

> **"If your brother sins [against you], go and tell him his fault between you and him alone. If he listens to you, you have won over your brother." (Matt 18:15)**

Confronting in Church

If you ever belonged to a group with a member who failed to "go with the program"—a team member of your basketball club who often missed practice, or a cast member who refused to learn his lines—you know the kind of situation addressed by this Sunday's Gospel. Of the five major speeches of Jesus in the Gospel of Matthew, the fourth one (from which today's reading comes) is about the internal management of the Church. One scholar called his study of this speech "Matthew's Advice to a Divided Community," because he saw in this passage the evangelist's focusing of Jesus' sayings to address problems of his own divided church.

In the center of Matthew 18 sits a procedure similar to the protocol mandated in almost any secular policy manual. For example, the student handbook at the school where I teach says that if you want to challenge a grade you should first take your case to the instructor. If the problem is settled at that level, fine. If not, take it to the department chair. If you find no satisfaction there, go to the dean.

This is a procedure for conflict resolution that thousands of reasonable persons have arrived at without consulting Scripture. What elevates this protocol to something worthy of the inner life of the Church is the context the evangelist provides. First, Matthew has carefully placed the parable of the shepherd and the lost sheep right before this disciplinary procedure. The story of the lost sheep, which in Luke 15 is a defense of Jesus' practice of eating with tax collectors and sinners, becomes in Matthew 18 a model for the exercise of Christian authority (go after the wandering sheep lovingly).

Then, right after the escalating procedure, which in the hard case can result in excommunication, Matthew describes this use of authority with the "binding and loosing" language used in Jewish circles to describe the chief rabbi's authority to include or exclude from community. It is the same language used of Peter's authority in Matthew 16:18. This grounds the authority in Christ. To further keep this disciplinary authority in perspective, Matthew next includes two powerful sayings that remind his readers that the community in which such discipline occurs is the same community whose power of petitionary prayer derives from their praying together and whose source of unity is the presence of the risen Lord in their midst (18:19-20).

Finally, Matthew rounds off the context of the confrontation protocol by completing the speech with another parable, the unforgiving servant—about a man who is forgiven something like our national debt and then turns around and abuses a coworker who owes him a mere pittance. The obvious message: if we have been forgiven enormously by God, we should pass on that forgiveness generously to our fellow human beings.

Thus, the evangelist takes one of the toughest challenges any community has to face—what to do with the recalcitrant member whose behavior endangers the life of the community—and presents a reasonable protocol of escalating confrontation; but he makes sure this is done in the spirit of Christ by surrounding it with teachings of Jesus modeling extreme care (shepherd parable), prayer, and endless forgiveness. What holds for pope and bishops extends, of course, to pastors, parents, teachers, employers, and friends.

Twenty-Fourth Sunday of the Year

Readings: Sir 27:30–28:7; Rom 14:7-9; Matt 18:21-35

> **"Forgive your neighbor's injustice;**
> **then when you pray, your own sins will be forgiven."**
> **(Sir 28:2)**

THE ACCOUNTANCY OF FORGIVENESS

Peter knew well what his master taught about forgiveness. It was especially clear in the model prayer Jesus had taught the disciples: "Forgive us our trespasses as we forgive those who trespass against us." That was clear enough; yet Peter's question was a very human one: "How far do I have to go in this forgiveness thing?" As an outside limit, he suggests the round number seven. Jesus (teasingly?) responds with the fuller round number seventy times seven—or 490, to be exact. And of course the point was that, like the lawyer who asked Jesus to define "neighbor" (looking for some boundary around the love commandment), Peter is wrong to inquire into the limits of the command to forgive.

Seeing that Peter wants to quantify forgiveness, Jesus tells a parable about forgiveness using numbers whose proportions are absurd. ("You want to talk numbers? I'll give you some numbers to think about.") Jesus tells of a king calling his debtors to account and dealing with one who owes him *ten thousand talents*. Now a single talent was a huge amount of silver, worth, our lexicons tell us, around 10,000 denarii (and a denarius was worth a day's labor). Thus, 10,000 talents would come to a hundred million denarii. If you like, you can estimate what a day's worth of labor is worth today in dollars and then multiply that by 100,000,000. But just trying to think of an amount worth the salary of 100,000,000 days' labor should be enough to help us realize that the NAB's paraphrase for "ten thousand talents"—"a huge amount"— while correct, is really an understatement.

When the king orders the debtor, along with his family and property, to be sold to recover a little of the debt, our debtor begs for mercy and makes the absurd promise that he will pay the debt "in full." The king overlooks the absurdity, allows himself to be moved by compassion, and forgives the man outright.

Still in the flush of what we must imagine would be a feeling of unexpected good fortune and gratitude, this liberated debtor runs into a coworker who owes him a mere hundred denarii (which comes to one millionth of what he had just been forgiven—in case Peter is still trying to imagine 490 instances of forgiveness). And the man has the gall to demand immediate payment. When the coworker pleads with our forgiven debtor *in the very words he had just used before the king,* the man has him committed to the debtors' prison. Knowing of the first man's recent benefit, the other servants are rightly enraged, as is the king, when he finds out.

Jesus' (satiric) numbers game answering Peter's (misguidedly serious) numbers game is there for us to contemplate, if we dare to measure how much the Lord would have us forgive one another.

Twenty-Fifth Sunday of the Year

Readings: Isa 55:6-9; Phil 1:20c-24, 27a; Matt 20:1-16a

"Are you envious because I am generous [Greek: Is your eye evil because I am good?]?" (Matt 20:15b)

GOOD GOD, EVIL EYE

In the parable of the householder and the vineyard workers, when the master pays the eleventh-hour people the same wage (a denarius, normal pay for a day's labor) that he pays to those who had borne the heat of the day, our sense of fairness is violated. We understand easily the grumbling of the full-day workers: if the one-hour workers get a full day's pay, should not they, in all fairness, get something like twelve days' pay? The householder's defense seems lame. The fact that the full-day workers had agreed to a denarius does not really address the apparent lack of proportion in the eleventh-hour workers getting for one hour's work what they ("the heat of the day" people) had worked so hard to earn. The householder may indeed be "generous" with respect to the eleventh-hour people, but in this situation, the full-day workers experience the normal day's wage as decidedly ungenerous. "Generous" would be something like maybe ten or twelve denarii.

But despite most contemporary English translations of the adjective the householder applies to himself in verse 15, the issue is not generosity but goodness. For a literal rendering of Matthew 20:15b (reflected accurately in the King James and the Rheims versions) reads: "Is your eye evil because I am good?" The importance of the difference between "generous" and "good" becomes apparent when we consider the fuller context.

This is, after all, not a teaching about just wages but a parable that begins, "The kingdom of heaven is like . . ." As readers of Matthew, by now two-thirds through this Gospel, we know that "kingdom of heaven" is not a name for the place where God lives but the realm of human

101

persons responding to God's reign freshly inaugurated through Jesus of Nazareth. As in other householder parables, the master is of course God. And the issue of God's goodness and what it takes to relate appropriately to that goodness is raised in the previous chapter, when a young man approaches Jesus and asks, "Teacher, what good must I do to gain eternal life?" And Jesus answers, "Why do you ask me about the good? There is only One who is good." In the ensuing conversation, Jesus says that following the commandments is doing "the good" but that full goodness, indeed "perfection," comes with letting go of everything and following him, Jesus. Relating to the ultimately good One, in other words, is converting to a new way of looking at and living one's life—i.e., receiving the teaching of Jesus and becoming his disciple.

When Peter follows this with his question about how he and the rest of the disciples will be rewarded for giving up all to follow him, Jesus speaks of reigning with him, enjoying the hundredfold and inheriting eternal life. But then, as if to disabuse the disciples (and Matthew's readers) of conventional notions of accomplishment and reward, Jesus launches into our parable about the householder. The parable flies in the face of normal expectations about accomplishments and reward, or work and wages. Perhaps the key lies in the master's agreement with the third-hour (9 A.M.) people to pay them "what is just" (NAB; or "whatever is right," NRSV). At this point in the story, we readers or listeners naturally take this to mean something less than the denarius promised the workers who started at dawn. When, along with the eleventh-hour people, we bristle at the news that all workers will be paid equally, we hear Jesus say, "Is your eye evil because I am good?" In the Mediterranean world, one of the things that makes for an "evil eye" is to look upon someone else's goods with jealousy—to make *invidious* comparison. The very word "invidious" (from Latin *invidere* "to look at with envy") derives from that understanding of evil eye.

As Isaiah reminds us in the first reading, God's ways are not ours; God's goodness would create a kind of equality in the household of the kingdom that goes beyond our small sense of "what is right." To the extent we make invidious comparisons—like Martha with Mary, or like the elder son with respect to his prodigal brother—to that extent our eye is evil and we are blind to the goodness of God.

Twenty-Sixth Sunday of the Year

Readings: Ezek 18:25-28; Phil 2:1-11; Matt 21:28-32

"Which of the two did his father's will?" (Matt 21:31)

DO IT!

To whom does Jesus address this sharp little parable of the two sons? In the preceding episode, Matthew states that they are the chief priests and the elders. On the day after Jesus' dramatic action in the Temple precincts, these high officials have come to challenge Jesus' authority for "doing these things," apparently referring to Jesus' clearing the Temple area and continuing to hold teach-ins on the Temple grounds (the officials' turf, so to speak).

Jesus turns the tables on his questioners. He asks "Where was John's baptism from? Was it of heavenly or of human origin?" Was Jesus dodging their question? No. He was exposing his questioners' hypocrisy. They were not making an honest enquiry in order to take a stand. Matthew makes this clear by telling us what the chief priests and elders said among themselves. "If we say, 'Of heavenly origin,' he will say to us, 'Then why did you not believe him?' But if we say, 'Of human origin,' we fear the crowd, for they all regard John as a prophet." So they say to Jesus, "We do not know." Thus Jesus' question has exposed the fact that these men are not really concerned about divine authority; they are simply maneuvering to protect their own power. Had they really been concerned about divinely given authority, they would have recognized it in John the Baptist.

Against that background, the parable of the Two Sons is clear. In the Scriptures, a vineyard is an image for Israel itself and the owner is God (e.g., Isaiah 5). If anyone is commissioned by the Owner to "go out and work in the vineyard," it is surely the religious leaders. When the chief priests and elders affirm that the one who did his father's will is the one who, though he initially said no, later goes to work, they condemn themselves, as Jesus spells out in his application (vv. 31b-32).

"When John came to you in the way of righteousness, you did not believe him; but tax collectors and prostitutes did." In this, the tax collectors are like the first son (the no/yes one); for in their former way of life, they were naysayers to the will of God, but they eventually did the will of God by responding in repentance to the preaching of John the Baptist. In one way, the leaders seem to reflect the performance of the second son, in that, as religious leaders, they were ostensibly keepers of the law of God. But, since the immediate context entails the responses first to John and now to himself, they are "none of the above." That is, the chief priests and elders have been closed to God's authority both when it was mediated by John and also now as it is mediated by Jesus. So they are worse than either of the two sons in the parable. Intent only on holding on to their own human authority, they have become hard of heart, unresponsive late and soon to God's mediators. Yet, Jesus' confrontation does not slam the door on his listeners. He says that the tax collectors and prostitutes are entering the kingdom of God *"before* you"—not *instead of* you. Conversion is always possible.

This parable gives us an insight into why "the poor" are congratulated in the first Beatitude. The religious leaders became distracted from acknowledging the authority of God and doing his will because of their attachment to the power of their human authority. Tax collectors and prostitutes, on the other hand, despite whatever minor financial and erotic power they may have possessed, were sufficiently aware of their limitations to be open to the power and authority of God when they encountered it in John and in Jesus.

Very likely, most of us feel we would have been among those who responded well to Jesus' exercise of authority, had we been alive in early first-century Galilee and Judea. It might be a good meditation for us to try to imagine how we would have responded to John the Baptist. Would we have given a good listening to that strange man of the wilderness, dressed in animal skin, snacking on locusts and inviting people to a dunking in the Jordan? Though John and Jesus were very different men—one a dedicated faster and the other dining regularly with tax collectors and sinners—those who were drawn to Jesus were the same ones who gave John a hearing.

Twenty-Seventh Sunday of the Year

Readings: Isa 5:1-7; Phil 4:6-9; Matt 21:33-43

> **"When the chief priests and the Pharisees heard his parables, they knew that he was speaking about them." (Matt 21:45)**

VARIETIES OF VIOLENCE

The day after Jesus' prophetic action in the Temple, when he was teaching in the Temple precincts, the chief priests and elders come to challenge his authority for "doing these things" (Matt 21:23). As part of his response, Jesus tells the parable about the wicked tenants. Matthew remarks, "They knew that he was speaking about them." How did they catch on so quickly? Jesus was drawing upon a prophetic tradition they knew very well.

This Sunday's first reading presents exactly the passage Jesus was alluding to in the parable, Isaiah's allegory of the fruitless vineyard. In that little masterpiece, the eighth-century prophet was addressing the leaders of his own day in a parable of his own. Israel's Lord is portrayed as a vineyard owner who is so intimately and caringly related to his vineyard that he images it as a marriage relationship. Finding, at harvest time, that the vineyard has produced no grapes, he takes it to the divorce court! In case his audience has missed the point, Isaiah explains, "The vineyard of the LORD of hosts is the house of Israel, / and the people of Judah are his cherished plant." And if they are wondering exactly how Israel/Judah was fruitless, he makes it clear that the problem is violence: "He looked for judgment, but see, bloodshed! for justice, but hark, the outcry!"

Jesus evokes Isaiah's parable by virtually quoting its first line: "There was a landowner who planted a vineyard, put a hedge around it, dug a wine press in it, and built a tower." He makes explicit Isaiah's hints about violence by expanding the parable into a story about tenants who beat up and kill the slaves sent by the owner to collect the produce. Jesus further updates Isaiah's parable by having the tenants kill the son of the owner outside of the vineyard, a clear reference to his own imminent death by crucifixion outside of the city.

Isaiah and Jesus both unveil violence. As the verses following Isaiah's vineyard parable make clear, that prophet had in mind the violence of an alcoholic lifestyle mixed with land-grabbing. Jesus, on the other hand, focused on Israel's violent rejection of its prophets (and finally of himself). As Jesus updates his eighth-century predecessor, can we contemporize Jesus' teaching? In our own day, our U.S. bishops have dared to unveil a kind of violence hidden for centuries and, until recently, little mentioned in official Church teaching—domestic violence, especially against women. In their pastoral letter, *When I Call for Help: A Pastoral Response to Domestic Violence Against Women* (1992), they state unequivocally that "violence against women, in the home or outside, is *never* justified. Violence in any form—physical, sexual, psychological, or verbal—is sinful; many times, it is a crime as well." The bishops note a study in the *Journal of the American Medical Association* claiming that "an estimated 3 to 4 million women in the United States are battered each year by their husbands or partners." Shockingly, "approximately 37 percent of obstetric patients—of every race, class, and education background—report being physically abused while pregnant." In addition to naming the violence, the bishops write out of a desire to offer the Church's resources to both the women who are battered and the men who abuse. "Both groups," they say, "need Jesus' strength and healing."

As we hear how Isaiah and Jesus address the violence of their own days, let's attend to the prophetic voice of our own bishops in this matter. The love of neighbor to which Jesus calls us urges us to be alert to the possibility of violence and near-violence in our own behavior with family members. That same love command calls us to be sensitive to signs of abuse and battering among people we relate to. And should any one of us find herself a victim of domestic violence, our leaders would have her know that the Church considers it part of its pastoral ministry to help. Let us not be afraid to reach out in this matter—either to ask for help or to give it.

Twenty-Eighth Sunday of the Year

Readings: Isa 25:6-10a; Phil 4:12-14, 19-20; Matt 22:1-14

"My friend, how is it that you came in here without a wedding garment?" (Matt 22:12)

THE GREAT FEAST, TOLD TWICE

The quickest way to understand the parable of the great feast in Matthew 22 is to first read Luke's version of the same story in Luke 14:16-24. Most students of the parables are convinced that, in this case, Luke gives us the version closest to Jesus' life setting and that Matthew has given the parable quite a different turn to apply it to the pastoral needs of the community for whom he was writing.

So read Luke 14:16-24 first. Notice that in his setting, a dinner party, Jesus tells the story in response to a guest's dreamy statement: "Blessed is the one who will dine in the kingdom of God." Jesus proceeds to tell of a banquet to which none of the invited guests come, all of them begging off with phony excuses. The would-be host then instructs his servant to invite the poor, crippled, blind, and lame. Finding that there is still room, he has the servant call people in from the highways and hedgerows. In Luke's setting, the parable is a commentary on Jesus' ministry and who is responding, or not. To his dreamy dining companion Jesus is saying something that might be paraphrased: "Buddy, the kingdom of God is not something in the distant future. In my own preaching and table fellowship I've been inviting people to the table of the kingdom of God regularly, but most of those invited reject me, coming up with excuses like, 'He eats with tax collectors and sinners,' or 'He heals on the Sabbath.' Meanwhile, it is the poor and those in need of healing who respond to my invitation to the reign of God. And even outsiders (Gentiles) will be included." Thus far Luke.

Matthew, on the other hand, has Jesus tell the story in the Temple precincts, when the chief priests and Pharisees come to challenge his authority after the clearing of the Temple. Matthew's fingerprints are all over his version of it. He specifies the characters and the occasion as a *wedding feast* that a *king* gives for *his son*—making it easy to identify God inviting the people of Israel to the eschatological banquet of his Son Jesus Christ. The single servant in Luke becomes *two groups* of servants in Matthew. More than simply excusing themselves, the invitees abuse and even murder the servants—all of which parallels the behavior of the wicked vineyard tenants of the parable placed just before this in Matthew's Gospel. So in Matthew's version, the two waves of servants easily fit the pattern of the former and the latter prophets (as in the story of the wicked tenants). In this version, the angry response of the host shows not only in the invitation of "street people" but in the destruction of those murderers and the burning of "their city."

By this time, the original readers would have caught the fact that Matthew has turned the parable into a mini-history of Israel, alluding first to the people's rejection of the prophets—both Hebrew prophets and Christian—then alluding to the (recent?) 70 C.E. destruction of Jerusalem by the Romans, interpreted as an act of God. The final scene, the king coming in to meet the guests gathered from the roads, is a "fast-forward" to the final judgment. If we are puzzled by the king's singling out a guest caught without a wedding garment, we miss the cultural note that the host of such a wedding feast would supply a closetful of festive garments for the guests, and it is this man's fault that he has not cooperated (none of the other "street people" seem to be lacking proper attire).

What was, in Luke, an illumination of Jesus' kingdom preaching ministry becomes, in Matthew's hands, a cautionary tale. As in the parables of the Weeds and the Wheat and the Net (both in Matthew 13), or the Wise and Foolish Bridesmaids and the Sheep and the Goats in Matthew 25, this is a parable about divine judgment aimed at a complacent community. Having one's wedding garment on is a symbol parallel to having your oil-lamp ready for the advent of the Bridegroom. It means having fed the hungry, having clothed the naked, having housed the homeless and so on, as in the vision of the sheep and the goats (Matt 25:31-46), where Jesus gives away the secret.

Twenty-Ninth Sunday of the Year

Readings: Isa 45:1, 4-6; 1 Thess 1:1-5b; Matt 22:15-21

"Whose image is this . . . ?" (Matt 22:20)

No Tax Break Here

A cartoon by Auth shows a roomful of partying politicians, elephantine and asinine alike. The legend declares, "At the Welfare 'Reform' Celebration . . ." Through a window you can see a forlorn youngster holding up a sign: "14 MILLION AMERICAN KIDS IN POVERTY." One of the pols notices and says, "Lighten up, kid. Nobody likes a sore loser."

Taxes, and how they are used, have always been a sensitive issue. The Pharisees and the Herodians are acutely aware of this when they approach Jesus with the question: "Is it lawful to pay the census tax to Caesar or not?" They figure they have him either way. Either a yes or a no answer will get Jesus in trouble. If he says no, they have grounds to accuse him of sedition before the procurator. On the other hand, a yes answer will make him unpopular with the people, who find the Roman tax burdensome. Jesus, however, refuses to give a yes or no answer. Instead, he calls for a denarius and asks whose image it carries. Hearing that it is Caesar's, he says, "Then repay to Caesar what belongs to Caesar and to God what belongs to God."

Most people, when they read or hear this response, think something like this: That is a clever answer, but now Jesus has left us with another difficult question: How do you sort out what is Caesar's and what is God's?

But that reaction misses the point of Jesus' remark. Lacking the cultural context, we miss two things. First, when Jesus asks for the coin (and one is promptly produced), he exposes the hypocrisy of his questioners. For any Jew who was sensitive to the demands of the Mosaic Law would not be carrying a coin embossed with the image of an emperor pictured as divine. The bearer of such a "graven image" has already settled for himself the question of relating to the Roman Empire and its economy.

Second, Jesus' question about whose "image" the coin carries contains an allusion that most of us miss. If an image on something indicates authority and ownership, and Caesar's image on the coin implies the dominion of the empire, *what bears God's image, indicating the ownership and dominion of God?* Anyone, especially any Jew, knew that human beings are created in the image of God.

Thus Jesus' response is not a clever dodge. It is a confrontation. The world is not divided into one part for God (however large) and one part (however small) for Caesar. All creation is, first of all, under God's sovereignty, especially human beings, who as God's image have a special role in stewarding the goods of creation. Then, within that context, one works out the smaller question of relating to the empire. Jesus' challenge to his adversaries, then, is that in refusing to deal with Jesus' truth, they are resisting the reign of God. They are failing to live out their roles as bearers of God's image.

The reading from Isaiah provides a powerful background for meditating on this Gospel. Isaiah presents the voice of God referring to another head of empire, Cyrus the Great, as his "anointed one." This pagan emperor of the Persians earns that title because he, albeit unknowingly, has become God's instrument in the restoration of the exiled Judeans to their homeland. As in the action and words of Jesus in the Gospel, God's role as Creator of all is very much in the picture. Before and after this reading, the prophet speaks of God as "the LORD, who made all things, / who alone stretched out the heavens, / when I spread out the earth" (Isa 44:24) and who "made the earth / and created mankind upon it" (45:12). Unlike Cyrus, the Pharisees and Herodians were failing to cooperate with the Creator of all.

Even in our own day, when we address the question of taxation, we can suffer from amnesia regarding the image of God borne by all humanity. We live in a culture that easily divides the world into three parts—one part (as much as I can get) for me and mine, another part (as little as possible) for Caesar, and, oh yes, a third part (as much as is left over) for God. Jesus would remind us that as creatures made in God's image, we are to use taxes as a tool for seeing that the goods of the earth are used to meet the needs of all. Not a popular notion at a time when the highest political value is not the common good but a tax break.

Thirtieth Sunday of the Year

Readings: Exod 22:20-26; 1 Thess 1:5c-10; Matt 22:34-40

"This is the greatest and the first commandment."
(Matt 22:38)

HOW TO LOVE GOD

The teacher of the Law thinks he is going to stump Jesus with his question about the greatest command, and Jesus answers simply by reciting the daily Jewish prayer called the *Shema* ("Hear!"). It is so named after the first word of Deuteronomy 6:4-9, which begins, "Hear, O Israel: The LORD is our God, the LORD alone. Therefore, you shall love the LORD your God, with all your heart, and with all your soul, and with all your strength." Jesus then goes beyond the question by quoting what he calls "the second": "You shall love your neighbor as yourself," which comes from another book of the Law, Leviticus 19:18.

What could be simpler? What could be more obvious? I trust that few, if any, Jews would disagree. And every Christian knows about this question and Jesus' answer. But my hunch is that most of us have oversimplified it. If you are like me, at some point in your life, you began to interpret Jesus' double love command in the light of another New Testament statement: "No one has ever seen God. Yet, if we love one another, God remains in us, and his love is brought to perfection in us" (1 John 4:12). Taken by itself, that verse seems to let us off the hook regarding the difficult business of loving an invisible God, and appears to call us to concentrate on loving the visible neighbor.

But of course it is not that simple. The context of 1 John 4 implies that the author is addressing people who think their profession of love of God has absolved them from attending to their neighbor's needs. In Jesus' response to the lawyer's question, however, he is quite clear that loving God is indeed the first and greatest commandment.

How, then, does one take seriously (and concretely and practically) the command to love the invisible God? Are all followers of Christ to

111

become monks? St. Ignatius (no monk) took this command with full seriousness and even dared to work out a set of "how-to" notes for himself and his companions. The notes comprise the final contemplation in his *Spiritual Exercises*—"Contemplation to Attain the Love of God"—referring not to God's love of us, which is always given, but our love of God, which always needs coaching.

Ignatius begins by calling the retreatant's (let's just say "our") attention to the simple reality that love consists more in deeds than in words, that lovers give what they have to one another. Then he instructs us to place ourselves in the presence of the Lord and the communion of saints and to ask the Lord to wake us up to a knowledge of the gifts we have received (from God, of course) and to stir up gratitude "so that I may become able to love and serve the Divine Majesty in all things." Now the simple insight begins to dawn: The most direct way we can obey the command to love God is to pay attention to God's gifts.

The remainder of the contemplation presents four concrete ways of getting in touch with those gifts of God. The first is, "I will call back into my memory the gifts I have received—my creation, redemption, and other gifts particular to myself." In other words, he suggests that we review our life story. Then he tells us to consider how much we ought to offer and give to God, suggesting at this point the famous "Suscipe" prayer, which begins, "Take, Lord, and receive all my liberty, my memory, my understanding, and all my will—all that I have and possess. You, Lord, have given all that to me. I now give it back to you."

The second way is to consider how God is present within all creatures—"in the elements, giving them existence; in plants, giving them life; in animals, giving them sensation; in human beings, giving them intelligence, and finally, how in this way he dwells also in myself, giving me existence, life sensation, and intelligence; and even further, making me his temple, since I am created as a likeness and image of the divine Majesty."

The third way focuses on how God works for me "in all the creatures of the earth." Finally, the fourth way considers how all good things I discover in and around me are but partial reflections of their source, God.

When we take the command to love God seriously as "the first and greatest," it is not hard to see how love of neighbor follows from this. When we learn to see all human beings as fellow creatures and co-recipients of God's gifts, we are enabled that much more to love them.

Thirty-First Sunday of the Year

Readings: Mal 1:14b–2:2b, 8-10; 1 Thess 2:7b-9, 13; Matt 23:1-12

**"Have we not all the one father?
Has not the one God created us?" (Mal 2:10)**

WHAT WOULD JESUS SAY?

This Sunday's Gospel, the first half of Jesus' diatribe against the scribes and the Pharisees, is a dangerous text. Through the past nineteen centuries, many Christians, reading the passage carelessly and out of context, have taken these words as a condemnation of Jews and Judaism and have allowed the language to fuel anti-Semitic thoughts and actions. In our own day, Matthew scholars have blown the whistle on this interpretation of the passage. What we have in Matthew 23, they insist, is not Jesus excoriating Jews in general but Matthew refocusing and elaborating sayings of Jesus to critique the Jewish leadership of his own day (post-70 C.E.). Matthew's purpose is to challenge the authorities of his own community to a more authentic leadership.

The scenario sketched by the recent scholarship goes like this. The author of the Gospel of Matthew is part of a Jewish Christian community. He is writing some time after the Roman destruction of the Jerusalem Temple (70 C.E.). With the demise of that institution, the Sadducees have lost their power base, and the Pharisees and their scribes have begun to emerge as the leaders of post-Second-Temple Judaism. Called by their followers "rabbi" ("my lord"), most of these leaders, we can reasonably assume, were good and earnest men. Now Matthew, part of an emergent Jewish sect of "Jews for Jesus" soon to be called *Christianoi*, works on a new edition of the Gospel of Mark to help his own community live the faith in their circumstances. When he comes to the brief passage in Mark where Jesus denounces the scribes for their love of honors, abuse of widows, and pious hypocrisy (Mark 12:38-40), he sees an opportunity to aim this critique of leadership against the leaders of the larger Jewish community of his own day, his purpose being at least twofold: first, to shore up the authority of his subgroup, the Christian Jews of that town (Antioch? we can only guess); and second, to contrast the Christian style of community life with that of the larger community that surrounds them.

And so Matthew draws from Mark 12 and also from the tradition of Jesus' sayings reflected in Luke 11:37-52 and presents what he is convinced is Jesus' message to the situation of his own community. What we have then—in both Jesus' setting and Matthew's—is a case of Jews denouncing Jews. Jesus was acting in the tradition of Israelite prophets confronting corrupt leaders in their time and place—as in today's first reading, where Malachi, a Levite, criticizes the corruption of some Levitical priests; Matthew is countering fellow Jews regarding the best way to live the Law. The whole Gospel of Matthew says the way to be faithful to the Law of Moses is to do it according to the way of Jesus— especially as expressed in the Sermon on the Mount. In chapter 23, Matthew spells out the implications regarding the proper use of authority.

Like Malachi and Jesus, Matthew denounces hypocritical leaders among his fellow Jews—Christian and non-Christian. To make his point about what the service of leadership should look like among the Jesus people, he caricatures its opposite in his portrait of the leadership of the "others."

In the spirit of Jesus' teaching about living as a community of disciples ("The greatest among you must be your servant," 23:11), Matthew insists that they should eschew the titles claimed by the leadership of the dominant group around them; they should reserve the title "father" for God and use "Rabbi" and "Master" only for the Messiah.

While courtesy and good order may justify the use of titles in the Church today, nothing can ever justify reverting to a reading of this passage that has too often nurtured virulent anti-Semitism. The message is directed to us, not to others. It is a vivid way of reminding us to practice what we preach and to use our authority for service of one another in the spirit of Jesus.

Thirty-Second Sunday of the Year

Readings: Wis 6:12-16; 1 Thess 4:13-18; Matt 25:1-13

"Therefore, stay awake, for you know neither the day nor the hour." (Matt 25:13)

WISDOM'S READINESS

Recently I was interviewed by phone on a local radio talk show. The occasion was the apparent crescendo of catastrophes in recent months —hurricanes, floods, earthquakes. And the leading question was: "Are these the end-times? Are these the final disasters predicted in the book of Revelation?" My answer: "According to the New Testament writers the end-times commenced with the advent of Jesus, especially after his death and resurrection. So we have been in the end-times for nearly two thousand years. As for the *end* of the end-times, the Bible gives us no clues for calculating that. The author of Revelation is more interested in how to face the future in the light of a past event—the Easter victory of the Lamb that was slain."

I won't try to reconstruct the entire interview, but it was enough to remind me that both Jesus and his New Testament interpreters are quite clear that the times and seasons of God's future end-time activity are none of our business. Mark 13:32 should be enough to make that clear: "But of that day or hour, no one knows, neither the angels in heaven, nor the Son, but the Father alone." The verse that follows tells us where our concerns should be focused: "Be watchful! Be alert! You do not know when the time will come."

All of which should help us appreciate the import of this Sunday's Gospel. Regarding the end—be it one's own death or the end of the world—the point is not the knowledge of *when* but the wisdom of *readiness.*

To hear clearly the parable of the wise and foolish "groomsmaids," it helps to have in mind what Matthew's readers would have known about Near Eastern marriage customs. First, the women—simply called "virgins" in the Greek—are not best described with the familiar rendering "bridesmaids," for the context suggests that they belong to the groom's party. The scenario appears to be the following. Since the wedding party would occur at the groom's house (or that of his father), the young women are part of his entourage sent out to form a welcoming party as he brings his bride home. The delay is likely due to the customary and ceremonious discussion of the bride-price with his father-in-law (the longer the delay, the greater the father's insistence on the worth of his daughter?).

Having reached the welcoming point, the ten settle down to wait, get drowsy, and fall asleep. When a voice heralds the approach of the groom, and presumably the bride, five (called "foolish") discover they are low on oil and run off to buy some. By the time the groom's entourage, accompanied by the five wise virgins, join the full wedding party, the foolish ones find themselves locked out. Their shout of "Lord, Lord, open the door" is answered by the chilling response, "Amen, I say to you, I do not know you."

The rest of Matthew's Gospel tells us all we need to know to hear the meaning of this parable. Like the parables that frame it, the story symbolizes something about living life in view of the final coming of Christ and what it means to be ready for that moment of joy (to be wise), or deserve judgment (to be foolish).

And what precisely does it mean to be ready in the way symbolized by the wise possession of oil? The scenario here in this fifth and last speech in Matthew is fully anticipated in the first speech, the Sermon on the Mount. There too we hear of people, who had even prophesied and healed in Jesus' name, shouting "Lord, Lord" and hearing Jesus say, "I never knew you." As in the groomsmaids story, we hear of wise activity (building on rock) and foolish activity (building on sand). The speech leaves no doubt that wisdom here means hearing the word of Jesus and doing it, and foolishness is failing to do so. Having enough oil parallels building on rock (disciplining one's anger, lust, and vengefulness, Matthew 5), running the household responsibly (24:45), investing one's talents fully (25:20-23), and doing the corporal works of mercy spelled out in the climax of this speech—feeding the hungry, quenching the thirsty, receiving the stranger, clothing the naked, visiting the sick and imprisoned.

The parables about the parousia of Christ have nothing to say about calculating the end, but they have much to say about living in readiness. The deepest wisdom and fullest readiness, it turns out, is to live chastely, honestly, nonviolently (Matthew 5), and to meet our neighbors' basic needs (Matthew 25).

Place yourself among the five wise women with the full jugs of oil. When the Lord comes, join the party. Now place yourself among the five foolish ones with next to no oil. When you hear of the Lord's arrival, dash to the mall to buy some, turn up at the party, and find yourself locked out. You have just done a meditation on heaven and hell. Reflect on what Matthew teaches regarding what it takes to live wisely.

Thirty-Third Sunday of the Year

Readings: Prov 31:10-13, 19-20, 30-31; 1 Thess 5:1-6; Matt 25:14-15, 19-21

> "*. . . so out of fear I went off and buried your talent in the ground. Here it is back.*" (Matt 25:25)

GOOD FEAR, BAD FEAR

Along with the Prodigal Son story, the parable of the Talents is one of those stories of Jesus that most people feel pretty sure they understand. "Get off your behind and practice your piano. Some day you'll be judged on how you used your talents," says a mother to her plugged-in child, confident that she has the backing of the Lord himself on this one. And I am confident she's right in that application. That dimension of the parable is so obvious that the Gospel word *talanton* (Greek for a huge monetary unit of silver coinage amounting to something like a lifetime's earnings) has entered our languages with the meaning "God-given ability." (Besides our English word, I find *le talent* in French, *das Talent* in German, *il talento* in Italian, and *el talento* in Spanish.)

And yet the parable is about much more than using our native abilities. In Matthew's context, Jesus' last major speech, the parable is addressed to Christian disciples, and the charge of the master of the servants is nothing less than the whole mission of the Church—living and spreading the Gospel, making other communities of disciples. The wherewithal for conducting the mission is symbolized by these huge cash amounts—five lifetimes' earnings, two lifetimes' earnings, one lifetime's earnings (they are all huge amounts). The servants are mandated to "work with" those amounts until the master returns. Two of the servants double what they have been given and are rewarded upon the master's return. The third does what seems, on the face of it, to be a pretty responsible thing. He keeps the talent safe by burying it securely in the ground and, at the time of accounting, returns it intact to his master. Knowing that the master expected more, the servant tries to justify his action by citing his fear of the master. (Apparently he did not fear the consequences of disobeying the master.) Maybe he figured it was better to risk that upshot than to risk losing the original deposit by "working with it" in ways that just might fail.

The story, then, is a wake-up call for Christians who think they are doing the Lord's will when they simply preserve intact what they have been given rather than venturing it in ways that will enable the talents (the faith?) to grow. The fear of the third servant has led him to opt for security first.

How odd, then, on this thirty-third Sunday of the year, to hear the reading from Proverbs praise the industrious and generous woman precisely for her *fear:* "Charm is deceptive and beauty fleeting; / the woman who fears the LORD is to be praised" (Prov 31:30). Whereas servant number three gets thrown into the outer darkness thanks to his fear of the master, the woman celebrated in the last chapter of Proverbs gets praised for fearing the Lord.

Is there something wrong with this picture? Not really. In the Hebrew Scriptures, "fear of the Lord" is a positive, even essential quality to be in right relationship with the Lord. Indeed, "The fear of the LORD is the beginning of knowledge" (Prov 1:7; see 15:33). In the context of Israel's Wisdom literature, fear of God is a profound awe of the Creator that frees one from the fear of anything or anyone else, and it energizes one to act justly and generously. The first and second servants were acting obediently according to that healthy fear, whereas the third servant was hobbled by a lesser, craven fear.

Pope John XXIII said something that has found its way into a contemporary icon by Lentz: "We are not on earth to guard a museum, but to cultivate a flourishing garden of life." I suspect that such a sentiment was rooted in a fear of God nurtured in a long life of prayer and service. At a moment when many were preoccupied with keeping the deposit of faith secure, Pope John called for a new venture of renewal and dialogue in our life of Christian discipleship and mission.

Christ the King

Readings: Ezek 34:1-2, 15-17; 1 Cor 15:20-26, 28; Matt 25:31-46

**"Then they will answer and say,
'Lord, when did we see you hungry or thirsty . . .
and not minister to your needs?'" (Matt 25:44)**

THE REAL MESSIANIC SECRET

Is Matthew's scenario of the Last Judgment a parable ("The Sheep and the Goats")? Or is it a straightforward description of how it will be at the end? To be sure, it has parabolic elements: a verse and a half describe the Son of Man sorting out all the nations as a shepherd separates sheep and goats (the nightly routine of shepherds keeping mixed herds; sheep like to sleep out in the open, whereas goats need shelter at night to keep warm). But the remainder comes across as direct description, which makes the flock/herd simile all the more attention-catching.

The reader of Matthew's Gospel has, after 25 chapters, become well-schooled in metaphors for the sorting out of divine judgment. The comparisons have been rich and many—wheat versus chaff, the fruitful tree versus the sterile one, the builder on rock versus the builder on sand, wheat versus weeds, good fish versus bad fish, those with wedding garments versus those not, the provident servant versus the abusive one, the groomsmaids with enough oil versus those caught short, those who work with talents versus the lone one who refuses to venture . . . and now those separated like (the more valuable) sheep from (the less valuable) goats.

This simile of a shepherd separating flock and herd is more than another convenient image for sorting. In the context of divine judgment, the image evokes the very passage partially given as this Sunday's first reading, Ezekiel's oracle about the true shepherd (Ezek 34:11-31). In that vision, the prophet pictures God personally shepherding the (heretofore poorly shepherded) flock of Israel and also judging between sheep and sheep. Tellingly, Ezekiel shows the Great Shepherd reprimanding those sheep who feed on the good pasture and then tread down the rest of the grass, those who drink of clear water and proceed to foul the water with their feet. "Therefore, thus says the Lord GOD: Now will I judge between the fat and the lean sheep" (34:20).

With the evocation of that vivid prophetic tradition, we can expect some talk about concrete human behavior, and we are not disappointed. What follows is one of the most famous recognition scenes in all of world literature. The assembly of all the nations get three surprises. First, the king and judge of all turns out to be . . . not some wielder of military or media might . . . but Jesus of Nazareth. The second surprise is that the sole criterion of judgment is how they have treated needy persons—those who are hungry, thirsty, estranged, naked, ill, or imprisoned. The final, shocking surprise is that the king has taken such treatment, be it aid or neglect, personally.

Scholars debate about the identity of the assembled *ethnē* ("nations"? "Gentiles"?) and "the least brothers." A close tracking of Matthew's language convinces some that *panta ta ethnē* means "all the Gentiles" (assuming that Israel, in harmony with some intertestamental Jewish traditions, receives a separate judgment). Then "the least ones," like the "little ones" in Matthew 18, are taken to refer to the Christian disciples. On this reading, the Gentiles are judged on their treatment of needy Christians (mainly Jewish at Matthew's time)—which would be an assurance to Christians. But it is also a warning that if the Gentiles are to be judged on that basis, all the more shall Christians be judged in that light.

Other scholars, noting that a parallel reference to final judgment at Matthew 16:27 describes the Son of Man repaying *each* according to his conduct, insist that the phrase *panta ta ethnē* in this Gospel includes the whole of humankind. They also understand "the least of my brothers" extending beyond the Christian community to include all needy persons. Either way, the challenge to Christian disciples is total.

While "nations" cannot be strictly construed in the modern sense of nation-state, the language surely names groups, not individuals only. At a time when our own powerful republic consumes a disproportionate amount of the planet's resources, defaults on its U.N. dues, and chooses not to ratify a nuclear test ban treaty signed by the majority of nations—might it not be timely to attend to the corporate dimension of the Gospel's language?

Imagine, meditatively, this judgment scene according to statistics from *World Almanac 1999* (counting just the living of course): 1.9 billion Christians, 1.1 billion Muslims, 747 million Hindus, 353 million

Buddhists, 907 million atheists and nonreligious, 15 million Jews, and a great variety of others. As the scene unfolds, note the surprise of all as the simple criteria of judgment are revealed. Do you find yourself surprised as well?